PENGUIN BOOKS

THE CROSS AND THE CRESCENT

ABOUT THE AUTHOR

Richard Fletcher recently took early retirement from the University of York. His *The Quest for El Cid* (Hutchinson/Knopf) won the Wolfson Award and the *Los Angeles Times* History Prize. *The Conversion of Europe: From Paganism to Christianity 371–1386 AD* (US title *Barbarian Conversion*) (Harper Collins/Henry Holt), was a bestseller in 1999. His most recent book, *Bloodfeud: Murder and Revenge in Anglo-Saxon England* (Penguin/OUP), was critically acclaimed on publication in February 2002.

RICHARD FLETCHER

The Cross and the Crescent

*The dramatic story of the earliest
encounters between Christians and Muslims*

PENGUIN BOOKS

PENGUIN BOOKS

Published by the Penguin Group
Penguin Books Ltd, 80 Strand, London WC2R ORL, England
Penguin Putnam Inc., 375 Hudson Street, New York, New York 10014, USA
Penguin Books Australia Ltd, 250 Camberwell Road, Camberwell, Victoria 3124, Australia
Penguin Books Canada Ltd, 10 Alcorn Avenue, Toronto, Ontario, Canada M4V 3B2
Penguin Books India (P) Ltd, 11 Community Centre, Panchsheel Park, New Delhi – 110 017, India
Penguin Books (NZ) Ltd, Cnr Rosedale and Airborne Roads, Albany, Auckland, New Zealand
Penguin Books (South Africa) (Pty) Ltd, 24 Sturdee Avenue, Rosebank 2196, South Africa

Penguin Books Ltd, Registered Offices: 80 Strand, London WC2R ORL, England

www.penguin.com

First published by Allen Lane 2003
Published in Penguin Books with a new subtitle 2004
3

Copyright © Richard Fletcher, 2003
All rights reserved
The moral right of the author has been asserted

Typeset by Rowland Phototypesetting Ltd, Bury St Edmunds, Suffolk
Printed in England by Clays Ltd, St Ives plc

To Emma Clark

Contents

List of Maps

– History, Stephen said, is a nightmare from which I am trying to awake. . . . What if that nightmare gave you a back kick?

James Joyce, *Ulysses*

Preface

This book was first suggested to me in the course of a conversation in October 1998, commissioned in June 2000, pondered during the following months, and written between May and December 2001. Its publication has been delayed for reasons beyond the author's control. It is intended as a neutral introduction to the story of a large and complicated, intricate and controversial set of relationships, which has assisted in shaping the world for many millions of people of diverse cultural attachments living today: no more, no less.

The origins of the book go back a good deal further than the dates just indicated. For many years I taught undergraduate courses on various aspects of the relations between Christianity and Islam in the Middle Ages at the University of York where I was until recently employed. Well before that, however, a formative experience in my own undergraduate career at Oxford had implanted the seeds of an interest in this cultural encounter. In my first long vacation in 1963 I visited Spain with friends and for the first time in my life gazed with wonder upon the mosque of Córdoba and the Alhambra of Granada: I returned from my holiday intent upon learning more about the culture which had produced these marvels. In the immediately following Michaelmas term I attended what were called 'classes' – they were actually informal discussion groups – on the theme of 'Christianity and Islam in the Middle Ages'. These classes were presided over by a triumvirate consisting of Richard Southern (then Chichele Professor of Medieval History), Samuel Stern and Richard Walzer. These three were sometimes joined by Albert Hourani or Lorenzo Minio-Paluello, occasionally both. Simply to rehearse the names of these immensely distinguished scholars is to be sharply reminded how very privileged we pupils were. I cannot speak for other members of the group, but I am pretty sure that in a callow, nineteen-year-old way I had no idea how fortunate I was to be among the audience for their wise, lucid and thought-provoking reflections. The classes took place at All Souls' College, if I recall correctly in Dr Stern's rooms. There were not enough chairs to go round, so we sat on the floor quite literally at the feet of these scholars and just listened to them talking, sometimes joining in to ask a question or even venture an observation. It was a mode of teaching which perhaps could not have been encountered in any other university in the Western world at that time and which would be altogether unthinkable in the conditions that govern academic life today. I still possess the yellowing pages of notes, random and scrappy though they are, which I jotted down in the course of that term, as a reminder of one of the most valuable pedagogic experiences of my life.

In the nearer past, I record my grateful thanks to Craig Taylor, for guiding my purchase and assisting my early operation of a new computer; also for directing my attention to Honorat Bouvet (see Chapter 5). To my kinswoman Emma Clark (to whom the book is dedicated) I am deeply indebted for finding time in a busy life to read the entire typescript and comment constructively upon it from a Muslim's perspective. In the light of her criticisms I have introduced many changes into my text; where I have neglected her advice it has never been without anxious hesitation. I am indebted once again to the editorial skills of Stuart Proffitt, exercised on this occasion on a text which he had not commissioned.

Dates are given in their AD form (sometimes today more neutrally expressed as CE or Common Era): plenty of reference books exist which furnish parallel lists of Islamic Hegira and Christian AD/CE dates. In my nomenclature I am aware that the coupling of the terms 'Christendom and Islam' is in a strict sense inaccurate: 'Islam' is a faith which may thereby be linked to 'Christianity'; 'Christendom' is a territory or culture or society which may thereby be linked to the *Dār al-Islām* or 'Abode of Peace', that portion of the world in which the faith and law of Islam prevail. If I have overlooked instances in which I have slipped into this error I ask the forgiveness of those readers who might find it offensive. Readers' attention is drawn to the Chronology, the suggestions for further reading and the notes identifying quotations in the text which are to be found towards the back of the book.

In writing this book I have not infrequently regretted that I could not have included some consideration of Judaism, as the third (but earliest) of the monotheisms of the medieval world, whose fortunes were inextricably intertwined with those of the other two. But that would have made a very different and much longer book.

Finally, a quick word about the title. I am aware that the crescent did not become widely current as a symbol of Islam until the Ottoman period. I am also aware that other authors have been struck by the appositeness of the phrase 'cross and crescent' as a title for works on this theme. In the preface to his novel *Summer Lightning* (1929) P. G. Wodehouse owned to the chagrin he felt upon learning that two novels of that name had been published in England, and three in the United States. I take my cue from him, and venture the modest hope that the present work will be considered worthy of inclusion among the Hundred Best Books called *The Cross and the Crescent*.

Nunnington, York
June 2002

I

Ishmael's Children

Islam is the faith of a single sacred text; Christianity, by contrast, of many texts. This contrast between mono-textual and multi-textual faiths has had very far-reaching consequences in the world's history. The sacred text of Islam is the Koran, revealed by God to his Prophet Muhammad and under human editorial hands taking on its fixed and final form, according to orthodox Islamic tradition, within about twenty years of Muhammad's death in the year AD 632. The many Christian texts are commonly found within the covers of a single volume, the Bible. Our word 'bible' is derived from the Latin *bibliotheca*, meaning 'a library', and that is exactly what the Bible is. Part of this library comprises a mass of myth, history, law, poetry, counsel and prophecy inherited from Judaism, in aggregate making up the Old Testament. The New Testament contains the earliest Christian writings in the letters attributed to St Paul and other leaders of the apostolic age; no less than four versions of the life and teaching of Jesus of Nazareth, each one slightly different from the other three; a narrative which finds its focus in the missionary activity of St Paul; and a work of apocalyptic prophecy unveiling the imminent end of the world and the Second Coming of the Messiah.

GAUL

Córdoba

Carthage
Kairouan

Fez

Tripoli

Rome

R. Danube

R. Dnieper

Black

Constantinople

Ephesus

Antioch

Jerusalem

Alexandria

SINAI

R. Nile

```
o       800 km
o      500 miles
```

—— Approximate boundaries of Islamic dominion c.730
━━ Approximate boundaries of Eastern Roman/Byzantine Empire c.730

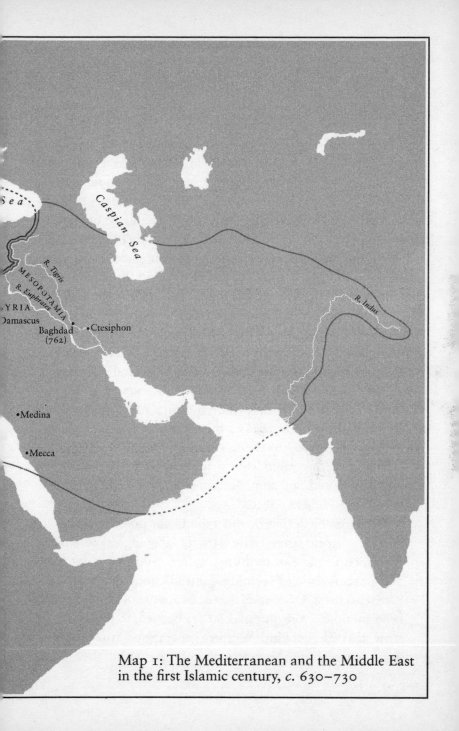

Map 1: The Mediterranean and the Middle East
in the first Islamic century, c. 630–730

This multiplicity and diversity of Christian texts, and especially of those letters and narratives bearing upon the teachings of Jesus and his earliest followers, have ensured that argument, debate and disagreement have been built into Christian history from its earliest traceable beginnings. From a certain point of view, Christian history has been about the sprouting of different tendencies or sects, about cellular fragmentations and re-formations, played out against a background din of polemic, denunciation and skulduggery. During the early Christian centuries the theological issues that generated the most intense and intemperate debates were the linked doctrines of the Trinity and the Incarnation. God is One, but He is also Three, the Father, the Son and the Holy Spirit. What precisely does this mean? What are the relations between these Three Persons of the Trinity? What does 'Son of God' signify? How could God be His own Son? In what sense was Jesus Man as well as God? These and related questions, obscure and difficult, exercised the best intellects of the Christian Church during much of the third, fourth and fifth centuries of the Christian era, and are still debated. In answer to them, theological definitions of great – and to the lay mind almost incomprehensible – subtlety were proposed. In some quarters these definitions were accepted; in others rejected.

Doctrinal bickering of this type is not possible under an Islamic dispensation. The strictly theological doctrines enshrined in the Koran do not suffer from the ambiguities and obscurities and seeming contradictions of the earliest Christian texts. Of course, that does not mean that Islam has been immune from internal strife, but it has tended to be strife of a different kind. Within a generation of the Prophet's death issues about the source of authority within the Islamic community had become divisive and would split that community between Sunni and Shi'ite factions in a rift that has never been healed.* The elaboration of a body of Islamic law from the Koran and the almost equally authoritative Hadith or 'Traditions' required interpretation, and rival schools of Islamic law established themselves in the course of time. Different commentators on these sacred texts advocated slightly different observances, slightly different forms and routines of piety. Individual holy persons experimented with new means of approaching God by way of asceticism or mysticism or communal activity, and their adherents formed groups or sects.

Holy men and sometimes – rather more frequently than is commonly believed – holy women might be revered within the *Dār al-Islām* (literally 'abode of peace', the lands in which the Islamic faith is observed and Islamic law prevails) as teachers, as spiritual guides, as being learned in the law. But they were not priests in the Christian sense. There is no priesthood in Islam. Nor is there, nor can there be, a Church in the sense of a religious institution set apart from the secular world, with its own organization, customs, staffing and funding. Authority within Islam is indivisible; there is no separation between the sacred and the secular. Under a

---

* The Shi'ites derive their name from the Arabic word *shī'at* meaning 'party' or 'faction' of Ali, who was both cousin and son-in-law of the Prophet. The Shi'ites refused to recognize the claims to authority of the first three caliphs who succeeded Muhammad, a refusal which precipitated civil war in the early Islamic community. The Sunnis on the other hand recognize and revere the early caliphs and attribute no special status to Ali and his descendants. At the present time Sunnis make up about 90 per cent of Muslims worldwide, the various Shi'ite sects the remaining 10 per cent.

Christian dispensation, on the other hand, there is a distinction between 'state', 'world', 'society' on the one hand and 'Church' on the other. The gap between them may be wide or narrow, relations between them warm or wary, but the distinction is always there, always containing the potential for tension and conflict.

These fundamental differences between Islam and Christianity have impeded easy understanding and harmonious dialogue. The austere monotheism of Islam finds the Christian doctrines of Trinity and Incarnation incomprehensible and distasteful. What else is a God who is in some sense 'divisible', a God who can turn himself into a man or a dove or a lamb, but some form of polytheism or idolatry, beliefs repeatedly condemned in the Koran? Christian sectarian divisions have traditionally been a matter for derision among Muslim onlookers. If there is a line of tension between Church and state (or society) within Christendom which there cannot be under Islam, that is going to open up completely different ways of thinking about authority and of organizing the community of the faithful – that is, of conducting politics.

By the time that Muhammad received his first revelations early in the seventh century, Christianity had been in law the exclusive faith of the Roman Empire, the superpower of the Mediterranean, for some two centuries. This does not mean that Roman authority and Christian belief were coterminous. Neither does it mean that the Christianity of the Roman world was either even or monochrome. Christianity had long been spreading beyond the political frontiers of the Roman Empire: by Muhammad's day exterior colonies of Christianity had been planted from Ethiopia to Ireland, Morocco to Georgia. Expansion had been most significant, both numerically and culturally, towards the east. A particularly flourishing branch of Christianity was to be found in Mesopotamia – roughly, modern Iraq – which was politically within the bounds of the other superpower of late antiquity, the Persian Empire. This 'Church of the East', as ecclesiastical historians call it – though 'Churches' in the plural might be more accurate – was already spawning missionary communities as far away as India and China.

Inside the Roman world the great cultural divide was that between east and west. The east – Greek-speaking, wealthier, more urbanized, comprising some of the great cities of antiquity (Alexandria, Antioch, Ephesus and the new arrival Constantinople) – was the more thoroughly Christianized. In the west – Latin-speaking, poorer, more rural, its provinces by now under the control of Germanic kings who had set up successor-states in the crumbling Western Empire of the fifth century – Christianity was still trying to make headway among a rural peasantry as yet little affected by it. The hectic doctrinal disputes already referred to had arrived at what appeared to be a resolution in a succession of Church councils culminating in the impressive meeting of nearly 600 bishops at Chalcedon, near Constantinople, in 451. However, the definitions of orthodoxy proposed there were unacceptable not only to the Churches of the east beyond the imperial frontiers and therefore unamenable to discipline, but also to a well-entrenched coalition of Christian sects inside the frontiers who could be, and were, coerced. These sects followed a doctrine of the Incarnation of Jesus known as Monophysitism, the belief that in the Incarnate Christ there was only one nature, not two (divine and human). The theological details need not concern us here: suffice it to say that the

Monophysites were thickly scattered through the eastern provinces of the Roman Empire from Armenia through Syria and Palestine to Egypt. Throughout the period from the late fifth until the early seventh centuries the Monophysites within the Empire experienced intermittent but sometimes intense persecution directed from the seat of orthodoxy in Constantinople.

The Arabs were the semi-nomadic tribespeople, sharing a common language and culture, who clustered along the frontiers of the two major imperial powers on the fringes of the Syrian Desert and were scattered in the habitable zones of the Arabian Peninsula proper.* The Arabs interacted with their two mighty imperial neighbours in all sorts of ways: seeking employment as mercenary soldiers; trading incense, camels or slaves to Syria or Mesopotamia; suffering capture and deportation as prisoners of war. Many of them stayed, willingly or unwillingly, within the empires into which they had made their way; some of them, as we shall see, rose to high positions in their new homes. There was traffic in the other direction too, for the frontiers of the empires were porous. Migrants from Rome or Persia settled among the Arabs, for example Jews or Christians who were fleeing persecution at home. By Muhammad's time there were plentiful Jewish and Christian expatriate communities in Arab lands, who diffused their faith and observance among the Syrian Arabs who were intrigued and attracted by these monotheisms of the Roman world. From the fourth century

* To clarify one small point which sometimes causes confusion: the Roman imperial province called 'Arabia' was confined to a fairly small territory lying, roughly speaking, between the Jordan Valley and the desert to the east. When St Paul referred to his sojourn 'in Arabia' (Galatians 1: 17), he did not mean what we call Saudi Arabia.

onwards there were communities of native Arab Christians in Syria, though not yet in the Arabian Peninsula, Churches which steadily grew throughout the fifth and sixth centuries and developed their own distinctive Christian Arab culture. Muhammad had himself travelled to Syria on business and numerous passages in the Koran attest his familiarity with both Judaism and Christianity.

The settled peoples of the two empires had that disdain for the Arabs that so frequently marks the attitude of the sedentary towards the nomad. Enmity between pastoralists and cultivators, the desert and the sown, goes back to Abel and Cain. Ammianus Marcellinus, last of the great Latin historians of antiquity, writing towards the end of the fourth century, is representative. He considered the Arabs a destructive people, who would swoop down like birds of prey to seize whatever they could find. And different in their habits too, not people like us: by means of what today would be called cultural stereotyping he distanced the Arabs as the unpalatable Other.

No man ever grasps a plough-handle nor cultivates a tree, none seeks a living by tilling the soil, but they rove continually over wide and extensive tracts without a home, without fixed abodes or laws . . . They wander so widely that a woman marries in one place, gives birth in another and rears her children far away . . . Wholly unacquainted with grain or wine, they feed on wild animals and milk and a variety of plants.[1]

Christian writers such as Ammianus' contemporary St Jerome, a near neighbour of the Arabs during his long residence at Bethlehem between 386 and 420, agreed with him. And these Christian authorities knew how to explain these peculiar people. It was all there in what the Bible had to say about Ishmael, whose birth and destiny are described in Genesis 16. Ishmael would be 'a wild man, his hand against every man's, and every man's hand against his; and he shall live at odds with all his kinsmen'. Here is Isidore of Seville, the great polymath and encyclopedist of late antiquity, and a contemporary of Muhammad, summing up a Christian consensus:

The Saracens live in the desert. They are also called the Ishmaelites, as the book of Genesis teaches, because they are descended from Ishmael [son of Abraham]. They are also called Hagarenes because they are descended from Hagar [Abraham's slave concubine, mother of Ishmael]. They also, as we have already said, perversely call themselves Saracens because they mendaciously boast of descent from Sarah [Abraham's legitimate wife].[2]

In this manner the Arabs could be marginalized as enemies of the human race by their tainted descent, or as we should say today by their ethnicity, as much as by the unappealing habits of nomads which were not those of the civilized world. And this had scriptural sanction. The word of God Himself in the Bible, it seemed, had declared that the Arabs should be outsiders for ever.

Dangerous people, unsavoury people, but useful so long as kept at arm's length. The East Roman imperial government set up a kind of buffer state among a Christian tribal confederation known as the Ghassānī Arabs (from an alleged ancestor Ghassān) whose zone of activity stretched along the eastern frontier from the Euphrates to Sinai. In return for subsidies, consideration and some of the trappings of sedentary power, the Ghassānīs did a good job of defending the frontier in the sixth century. But then something went wrong, and it is not wholly clear what. Perhaps the Ghassānīs were thought to be getting too independent. Perhaps it was that bureaucrats in Constantinople were looking to make economies. For whatever reason, the Ghassānī subsidy was cut. Offence was taken, relations ruptured. The eastern frontier lay vulnerable to Rome's traditional enemies, the Persians. The two powers fought themselves to an exhausted standstill in a long and ruinously expensive war between 603 and 629. Another consequence of the breach with the Ghassānīs was a hiatus in the gathering of political intelligence. The Ghassānīs had kept the imperial government well informed about developments in the Arab world. But in the early seventh century Constantinople fatally lost touch with what was going forward far to the south in Mecca and Medina.

The canonical account of early Islam has Muhammad receiving the divine revelations embodied in the Koran from 610, beginning to preach to the people of Mecca in about 612, encountering opposition and fleeing to Medina in 622, the latter event, the *Hijrah* or Hegira (literally 'migration') marking the beginning of the Islamic chronological era. Military victories won by the Anṣār, or 'helpers', his Medinan allies, enabled Muhammad to conquer the Meccans in 630. By the time of his death, traditionally dated to 632, it is claimed that most of the Arabs of the western parts of the Arabian Peninsula had submitted to his prophetic leadership and joined the *umma*, or community of believers, animated by the ideal of *islām*, or submission to the will of Allah. This traditional account bristles with all sorts of difficulties because the sources, if impartially evaluated, really tell us very little that is reliable about the Prophet's life and beliefs. That conceded, it is reasonably clear that Muhammad did not think that he was 'founding a new religion'. The phrase would probably not have made any sense to him. He had been chosen by the one true God as the Messenger who might bring the fullness of divine revelation, partially granted to earlier prophets such as Abraham, Moses or Jesus, to the Arabs of the Arabian Peninsula and thereby coax them away from their traditional polytheism and idolatry. The Messenger was essentially a Reminder:

> . . . it is a Reminder
> (and whoso wills, shall remember it)
> upon pages, high-honoured,
> uplifted, purified,
> by the hands of scribes noble, pious.[3]

The Messenger should remind people before all else of the imminence of the great and terrible judgement of God:

The unbelievers say, 'The Hour will never come to us.' Say: 'Yes indeed, by my Lord, it shall come to you, by Him who knows the Unseen: not so much as the weight of an ant in heaven and earth escapes from Him . . .'[4]

Those who had submitted – which is what the word *muslim* means – were required to live their lives on new lines. They must observe five fundamental disciplines, known as the five 'pillars of Islam': affirmation of God, daily prayer, fasting, almsgiving and pilgrimage, with their accompanying rituals. Commands and prohibitions, such as the ban on the drinking of wine, furnished additional struts for the framework within which the devout should live a righteous life. Much of the traditional ethic of the Arabs was retained under the new dispensation: matrimonial custom, for instance, or worship at the Kaaba at Mecca, or the duty of hospitality to strangers. But there were significant new departures. Muhammad brought a message of peace. The *umma* was a community bigger than the tribe, demanding a loyalty which came before loyalty to kinsfolk. Muslim must not fight against Muslim. There could be no return to the constant inter-tribal violence of raiding and vendetta which had characterized the pre-Islamic Arab world. Instead, a Muslim must practise *jihād*, a frequently mistranslated term meaning 'effort' or 'struggle' to convince unbelievers of the way of Islam. Such effort might be peaceful, the living of an exemplary pious life, the undertaking of teaching and preaching; but it might also be coercive and violent, should the unbelievers be stubborn.

After Muhammad's death – possibly even before it – Muslim armies began to campaign in the settled lands bordering the eastern Mediterranean. From one perspective, these were simply raiding operations of the type traditionally inflicted by one Arab tribe upon another but now forbidden by the code of the *umma* and therefore necessarily turned upon outsiders. From another, and more controversially among scholars, the campaigns were motivated by the desire to integrate all the Arabs into the *umma* and to establish it in the holy city of Jerusalem, there to await the imminent end of the world.

Whatever the truth about the underlying impulses, the events that followed are well known and well documented. Within twenty years of the Prophet's death the Muslims had laid hold of large parts of the Roman Empire and had wholly absorbed the Persian. The map of the Middle East would never be the same again. The story may be outlined very quickly. After scrappy raiding in Syria and Palestine the Muslims succeeded in capturing the city of Damascus in 635. In the following year they decisively defeated a Roman relief army at the Battle of the River Yarmuk: this victory laid the whole of Syria and Palestine at their feet. In 638 Jerusalem surrendered to them, in 640 Caesarea. Meanwhile, raiding eastwards into the Persian Empire had likewise been succeeded by a crushing Muslim victory in 637 and the subsequent capture of the capital city of the Empire, Ctesiphon. The last Persian emperor of the Sassanian dynasty retreated into his north-eastern territories, beyond the Caspian Sea, whence he conducted an ever-feebler rearguard action until his death in 651. Muslim armies had already turned their attention to the fabulously rich provinces of Egypt, at the end of 639. The same pattern of raids followed by victory in battle and the capture of major cities was repeated: Roman forces were defeated in the field in 640; Alexandria fell in 642, and with its fall came an end to six-and-a-half centuries of Roman rule. The advance continued westwards: Tripoli fell in 643. Further expansion westward was a good deal slower and more laborious, partly because the Muslims were weakened by the divisions between Sunni and Shi'ite in their own ruling circles, partly because in the Maghrib (north-west Africa) they came up against determined opposition from the indigenous Berber tribes of the region. A new garrison city was established at Kairouan in Tunisia in 670, and from there raids were regularly despatched westwards. These could be large-scale, long-range operations. One of them even penetrated to the coast of Morocco in 681, allowing the wondering eyes of the Arabs to gaze for the first time upon the waters of the Atlantic – though they were ambushed by Berbers on their way back and their leader killed. The last significant imperial stronghold, Carthage, fell to the newcomers in 698. Every vestige of effective Roman power had now been banished from North Africa. Next it was the turn of Europe. Raids across the Straits of Gibraltar were taking place from the early years of the eighth century, to be followed by a full-scale military invasion of Spain in 711. At a decisive battle at a site which has never been confidently identified, the Spanish king Rodrigo was defeated and killed; his capital city of Toledo was occupied shortly afterwards. The entire Iberian Peninsula was in the hands of the new masters by 718, at which time Muslim armies in the east were laying siege to the imperial capital, Constantinople itself. Shortly after this the conquerors of Spain began to despatch raiding parties across the Pyrenees into the southern parts of Frankish Gaul. Where, if anywhere, were the conquests going to stop?

The speed of the Islamic conquests, and especially the early ones in the 630s and 640s, has always astounded and puzzled historians. Both the empires of Rome and Persia were suffering from war-weariness and financial exhaustion. The Mediterranean world as a whole may have been weakened by demographic decline and prolonged economic recession caused by outbreaks of bubonic plague in the sixth century. The Arabs had talented generals, desert-hardened warriors, unquenchable morale and the priceless asset of mobility in the face of enemies whose armies were accustomed to slow-moving warfare. To the provincials of Syria and Palestine, who had experienced severe disruption in the long conflict between Rome and Persia, the armies of Muslim Arabs could have seemed like successors to the Ghassānīs, people who might become their protectors under treaty with the emperor, people therefore with whom it was prudent to make terms. To the persecuted Monophysite Christians of Syria and Egypt the Muslims could be presented as deliverers. The same could be said of the persecuted Jews of Spain.

We can take all these, and other, factors into account: but a satisfactory modern explanation of the initial expansion of Islam remains elusive. Contemporaries were less bewildered. Patriarch Sophronius of Jerusalem – he who negotiated the surrender of the city to the Muslims in 638 – explained the invasion of Palestine as divine punishment for the sins of the Christians. The notion that the Muslims were the instruments of God's wrath would have a long life. So too would the portrayal of Muhammad as a man of blood and of his followers as irredeemably violent. This first appears in a Christian work known as the *Doctrina Jacobi nuper baptizati* [The Teaching of Jacob the Newly-baptized], a tract of anti-Jewish polemic cast in dialogue form composed probably in Palestine round about the time of the surrender of Jerusalem. At one point the following words are attributed to one of the speakers, 'Abraham', a Palestinian Jew:

A false prophet has appeared among the Saracens … They say that the prophet has appeared coming with the Saracens, and is proclaiming the advent of the anointed one who is to come. I, Abraham, referred the matter to an old man very well-versed in the scriptures. I asked him: 'What is your view, master and teacher, of the prophet who has appeared among the Saracens?' He replied, groaning mightily: 'He is an impostor. Do the prophets come with sword and chariot? Truly these happenings today are works of disorder … But you go off, Master Abraham, and find out about the prophet who has appeared.' So I, Abraham, made enquiries, and was told by those who had met him: 'There is no truth to be found in the so-called prophet, only bloodshed; for he says he has the keys of paradise, which is incredible.'[5]

Notable here too is the tendency to interpret Islam in a biblical perspective (anointing, keys) and its Prophet as false, a deviant from Christian orthodoxy. Just as Isidore (and many later authors) could explain the Arabs as descendants of Ishmael, so it made sense to 'place' Muhammad as a Christian heretic.

Islam emerged at a time when the intellectual life of Christendom within the Roman world was focused very nearly exclusively upon the Bible and its expositors. Little by little, over the previous three centuries, the secular learning of antiquity had been eased off the syllabus of studies and the dominant culture of Christendom had taken on an ecclesiastical hue. This conditioned the Christian reaction to Islam in important ways. The idea that Islam might be 'a new religion' was in the strict sense of the term unthinkable: the thought could not have occurred. People can entertain the notion of 'a new religion' only when they are accustomed to the idea of religious pluralism, the idea (which we take for granted today) that among humanity there are many different religions. But the age of Isidore and Sophronius was not so accustomed. It was not until many centuries later that the first faint dawnings of the notion of a plurality of faiths stole over Christendom's horizon (see Chapter 4). Before that the certainties were grand and simple. There was The Faith, which was Christian. Of course, there were peoples visible who were not, or not yet, Christian, but they presented no challenge to the understanding. The Jews had been offered the faith but had rejected it; for this terrible sin of rejection they would one day suffer the consequences. There were pagans scattered all over the map, from Persian Zoroastrians to the rural peasantry of the Mediterranean hinterland who still worshipped springs and trees; but the Bible, God's word, was positive in its assurance that all these would one day be gathered into the Christian fold. So whom did that leave? Manifestly, the deviants from Christian orthodoxy, those who had wilfully chosen to go their own way, the heretics. (The primary meaning of the Greek word *heresis* is 'choice'.)

Muhammad and his sect were most plausibly understood as yet another wave of theological deviants who had gone astray on crucial matters of doctrine, like Monophysites and others. (Let us remember that it is only with hindsight that we can claim that Trinitarian controversy had been ended by the definitions of Chalcedon in 451.) There was so much that Muslims believed, or did, that was familiar to Christians. They believed in one God. They revered patriarchs, prophets and kings of the Old Testament – Abraham, Isaac, Jacob, Moses, Elijah, David, Solomon. They venerated the Virgin Mary, to whom indeed one of the chapters or *sūras* of the Koran is devoted (Sura 19). Respectful references to Jesus and his teaching occur repeatedly in the Koran. Like Christians they prayed and fasted, gave alms and went on pilgrimage. But they denied the Trinity, the Incarnation and the Resurrection; their holy book was a parody of sacred scripture; they exalted a pseudo-prophet; they made war on the Christians; and they had seized their Holy Places.

These early reactions to the phenomenon of Islam were transmitted to the most distant parts of Christendom. Few churchmen could have been further from the Muslim heartlands than Bede, monk, biblical scholar and historian of the coming of Christianity to the English, who lived, worked and in 735 died in the monastery of Jarrow in Northumbria. Yet Bede knew what needed to be known of the Saracens. In a work of biblical commentary completed in 716 he could describe them as 'enemies of the Church'. Four years later, commenting on the Ishmael reference of Genesis 16, he quoted St Jerome on the Saracens and went on to say:

But now is 'his hand against all and the hands of all against him' to such an extent that they oppress the whole of Africa with their domination and, odious and hostile to all, they control the greater part of Asia, and even part of Europe too.[6]

In his *Ecclesiastical History*, completed in 731, Bede drew attention to 'the very terrible plague of Saracens'[7] who were ravaging southern Gaul. Some English people's lives were directly affected by that Saracen presence. It was at much the same time that Boniface, the great English missionary to Germany, wrote home to an English friend, a nun, advising her to postpone her planned pilgrimage to Rome because of 'the raids and turbulence and menace of the Saracens which have been going on lately'.[8]

Initial Christian reactions to Islam, then, consisted of attempts at explanation within the constraints of biblical exegesis and theological orthodoxy, the whole flavoured with hostility. It is a good deal more difficult to gauge early Islamic reactions to Christianity. As we have seen, the pre-Islamic Arabs were well acquainted with both Judaism and Christianity, the major monotheistic religions of western Asia and the Mediterranean world. Some historians, relying on anthropological models derived from the observation of religious conversion in modern Africa, have suggested that changes in the material and moral culture of the Arabs in late antiquity may have made them ripe for the transition from polytheism to monotheism. Given the sparsity of the evidence, this is an argument that can only be suggested, not demonstrated. Quite large numbers of Syrian Arabs had already made that transition to the monotheism of Christianity before Muhammad's day. Questions of what may loosely and cautiously be called a political order raise their heads in this context. In matters of religious allegiance there was more at stake than simple confessional conviction. Choices had strings attached. To accept the faith of a superpower was in some sense to acknowledge and submit to a dominant culture. The Christian faith, about the year 600, was intimately bound up with East Roman order and authority. Islam offered the Arabs a monotheism of their own, with scriptures in their own language, holy places in their own heartlands and their own ways of setting about worship and devout living.

The Koran requires that Muslims should respect the *Ahl al-Kitāb*, the 'People of the Book', that is to say Jews and Christians:

Dispute not with the People of the Book save in the fairer manner, except for those of them that do wrong; and say, 'We believe in what has been sent down to us, and what has been sent down to you; our God and your God is One, and to Him we have surrendered.'[9]

The earliest biography of Muhammad contains a story about the recognition of the young man's prophethood by a Christian monk named Bahira. In the written traditions of Islam, therefore, there is an embedded cordiality towards Christianity. In practice, of course, this was not always observed. Patriarch Sophronius lamented the destruction of churches and monasteries which occurred during the Muslim invasion of Palestine. Such things happen in wartime. But the record of such capitulation treaties as survive shows that the leadership sought to observe Koranic precept. Christians and Jews should be allowed the free practice of their religion, under certain conditions. These *ahl ad-dhimmah*, or 'protected peoples' (sing. *dhimmī*), had to pay an annual poll tax. They were required to identify themselves by the wearing of a distinctive sash, or belt, known as a *zunnar*. They were not allowed to build new synagogues or churches, or to indulge in obtrusive religious practices such as ringing bells and public chanting. They were not permitted to possess certain items of military equipment. Sexual relations between *dhimmī* males and Muslim women were forbidden, as was, and very strictly, any showing of disrespect for Islam or attempts to convert Muslims to a different faith.

There was an overriding practical reason for the Islamic leadership to remain on friendly terms with the Christian populations of the lands they conquered. Not only did the conquered peoples vastly outnumber their conquerors; in addition, only Christians commanded the necessary administrative expertise to make government possible. Let us remember that the Arabs, barely acquainted with anything that we should recognize as government, in blundering into the eastern provinces of the Roman Empire were entering a world of considerable institutional sophistication. The superstructure of the empire had rested on a plinth of taxation, officials and written records. The Muslim conquerors made no attempt to displace what they found. How could they have done? They had neither the manpower nor the skills;

and they needed revenue. The conquered provinces, accordingly, ran in the same old way. Only the masters had changed. The early Islamic Caliphate – and the Arabic *khalīfa* simply means 'successor' (to the Prophet) – based at Damascus from 661 to 750 was, in an institutional perspective, no more than a successor-state to the Roman Empire.

A vivid illustration of this point is to be found in a narrative concerning the travels and tribulations of a party of English pilgrims to the Holy Places in the year 723. The leader of the party was a man named Willibald, a native of the Anglo-Saxon kingdom of Wessex, later bishop of Eichstätt in Germany, where he dictated his memoirs many years later in extreme old age. When the pilgrims landed in Syria after the sea-crossing from Cyprus they were arrested as spies and imprisoned. Let Willibald take up the story himself:

Then whilst they were still languishing in prison a man from Spain came and spoke with them inside the prison itself and made careful enquiries about their nationality and homeland . . . This Spaniard had a brother at the royal court, who was the chamberlain of the king [i.e. the caliph] of the Saracens. And when the governor who had sent them to prison came to court, both the Spaniard who had spoken to them in prison and the captain of the ship in which they had sailed from Cyprus came together in the presence of the Saracens' king, whose name was Emir al-Mummenin [perhaps an attempt at Amir al-Mu'minīn, a caliphal title meaning 'Commander of the Faithful']. The Spaniard told his brother all that he had learned about them, and he asked his brother to pass this information on to the king to help them. So when all these three came to the king and mentioned their case, telling him all the details from first to last, the king asked whence they came. They answered: 'These men come from the west where the sun sets; we know nothing of their country except that beyond it lies nothing but water.' Then the king asked them, saying: 'Why should we punish them? They have done us no harm. Allow them to depart and go on their way.'[10]

The interest of this little vignette for present purposes is that within five years of the completion of the conquest of Spain a native of Spain, presumably a Christian, had risen to a very exalted and responsible position in the central government of the caliphate at the other end of the Mediterranean. One would like to know more of the man's story. The rulers of the Islamic state had need of able administrators such as him.

By good fortune we are able to trace something of the history of a veritable dynasty of such administrators. A man named Mansur had resided at Damascus to administer the taxation of the Syrian provinces in the time of the Roman Emperor Heraclius, who ruled from 610 to 641. His name, Mansur, was Arabic; it means 'victorious'. Mansur evidently belonged to one of the Christian Arab communities settled within the Empire. He was an important official of high rank; one of the topmost figures, indeed, in the civil service of the Eastern Empire. Mansur had a son, Sergius, who followed in his father's footsteps as a fiscal mandarin. However, the authority he served was no longer the Christian emperor in Constantinople, but the Muslim caliph in his home city of Damascus, which had fallen into Arab hands, as we have seen, in 635. Sergius too had a son, named Mansur after his grandfather, who followed in the family tradition as an official in the public service. But here the chain of continuity was broken. In middle life the younger Mansur experienced a religious vocation and turned from his worldly life and successful career to become a monk in the famous monastery of St Saba, founded in the fifth century and still flourishing in the twenty-first, in the desolate country between Jerusalem and the Dead Sea. He took the name-in-religion of John, and it is as John of Damascus that he is remembered today as one of the Doctors of the Church. (After their release from captivity Willibald and his companions visited St Saba in the course of their tour of the Holy Places a few years after John's entry to the monastery: it is not impossible that the two men met.)

John was a prolific writer of theology, sermons, exegesis and hymns (some of the latter still sung in the English-speaking world in the translations of J. M. Neale). He was also the earliest Christian writer to concern himself at any length and in a systematic way with Islam. At some date unknown he composed a *Dialogue between a Saracen and a Christian*; and towards the end of his life, in about 745, he compiled a kind of encyclopedia of theological dissidence, *On Heresies*, which includes an entry on 'the superstition of the Ishmaelites'. The *Dialogue* envisages a situation in which a Muslim puts awkward questions to a Christian on such matters as the nature of Christ, creation, free will and so forth. The Christian parries these questions so skilfully that, in the work's closing words, 'the Saracen went his way surprised and bewildered, having nothing more to say'.[11] It is a kind of textbook of disputation, though it is difficult to envisage circumstances in which it could have been put to practical use. The section in *Heresies* on the superstition of the Ishmaelites is rather more interesting, as containing in embryo some themes that would occur again and again in Christian anti-Islamic polemic. John first explained the biblical derivation of the Ishmaelites. Then he went on to castigate Muhammad as a false prophet who cribbed part of his teaching from the Old and New Testaments and also from the sayings of a heretic Christian monk (i.e. Bahira). Muhammad wrote down 'some ridiculous compositions in a book of his',[12] which he claimed had been sent down to him from heaven. John then went on to ridicule certain Islamic doctrines or practices and to tell scurrilous stories about Muhammad. In thus mocking the faith of the Ishmaelites John quoted at some length, but selectively, from the text of the Koran. He evidently had access to it, or at any rate to extracts from it, in the monastery of St Saba where he wrote. We should very much like to know how he acquired such access.

The history of the family of John of Damascus offers us some fascinating glimpses of the range of Christian responses to the new arrivals. Here were three generations of exalted civil servants, of ethnically Arab origin, who could supervise the taxation of Syria successively for the emperor in Constantinople and for the caliph in Damascus. The implication is that for them the Islamic successor-state was as legitimate, as worth serving, as its predecessor. A bureaucrat's job was to keep the show on the road. Yet as a Christian writer John would mock and revile his former employers. We must not make too much of this: the anti-Islamic polemic constituted only a tiny proportion of John's entire literary output. But the attitudes it expressed were widespread. John's *On Heresies* was not just for home consumption in the monastery of St Saba. The work was dedicated to an old friend, Bishop Cosmas of Maiuma, the port for Gaza, a city whose Christian community remembered with pride and sorrow the martyrdom of its Roman garrison at the hands of the Muslim conquerors a century beforehand.

If John was so contemptuous of the new dispensation, why

did he not take the road of voluntary exile, as many another had done, to a safe haven within what remained of the embattled Roman Empire? There is another twist to the story here. About the time that John experienced his vocation the emperors in Constantinople had embarked upon a highly controversial policy of iconoclasm, the destruction of religious images. John was a vehement and eloquent upholder of the value of images – in fresco, mosaic, sculpture – as an aid to Christian worship. Living where he did, beyond the reach of the imperial authorities, he was safe from persecution. Had he returned to the Empire he would have lost certainly his liberty, perhaps his life. As it was, all that the Roman authorities could do was to shriek abuse at him:

Anathema to Mansur, the man of evil name and Saracen sentiments! Anathema to Mansur, the worshipper of images and writer of falsehood! Anathema to Mansur, the insulter of Christ and traitor to the Empire![13]

Thus the bishops assembled at the strongly iconoclast Church council of Constantinople in 754, shortly before John's death.

Echoes of similar ambiguities of allegiance are to be heard, if more faintly for shortage of documentation, in the most westerly of the Islamic conquests, the Iberian Peninsula. Our most important source of information about the age of the conquest is a set of annals known as the *Chronicle of 754* (because the final entry was composed in that year). The anonymous author wrote in Latin and may have been a cleric of Toledo, the capital city of both Church and state under the Visigothic kings who had ruled Spain as one of the most romanized of the successor-states to the Western Empire.

He deplored, sometimes movingly, the disruptions of the conquest and its aftermath in the generation after the initial invasion of 711–12. Like John's family, however, he seems to have accepted the legitimacy of the new masters. He even used their dating system alongside that with which he was familiar:

In the Era 767 [= AD 729], in the eleventh year of the [Roman] Emperor Leo and the one-hundred-and-twelfth year of the Arabs, the seventh year of [the Caliph] Hisham, Uthman came secretly from Africa to take over the government of Spain.[14]

Like John, he never referred to the new arrivals in terms other than ethnic. No more from him than from the eastern authors do we get even a hint that an entirely new religious culture had elbowed its way on to the Mediterranean scene. He gives the same sense of reassuring cultural continuity:

At that time Fredoarius bishop of Guadix, Urban the elderly chanter of the cathedral see of the royal city of Toledo, and archdeacon Evantius of the same see, were looked on as brilliant in their teaching, wisdom and sanctity, strengthening God's Church with faith, hope and charity, in all things in accordance with the scriptures.[15]

We also find in Spain, just a little bit later, an analogous treatment of Islam's Prophet. This occurs in a very short work known as the *Ystoria de Mahomet* composed probably in southern Spain in the eighth or early ninth century. Muhammad, 'a son of darkness',[16] stole some Christian teaching and claimed to be a prophet. He put together an absurd farrago of doctrine delivered to him by a vulture claiming to be the angel Gabriel. He incited his followers to war. He was a slave to lust, which he justified by laws for which he falsely claimed divine inspiration. He foretold his resurrection after his death but in the event his body was fittingly devoured by dogs. Like John of Damascus, the anonymous author was not ignorant of Islam and could make what appear to be fairly recondite references to the Koran. For example, 'he composed certain sayings about the hoopoe'[17] seems to be a reference to Koran 27:20. However, also like John, the author was embittered by hatred and contempt. In Spain as in Syria, Christians could accept and work with a new regime while covertly reviling the people who presided over it.

During the initial phase of Islamic expansion the conquerors held themselves aloof from their subject peoples. In general they did not settle widely in the conquered territories but were deliberately concentrated in big garrison cantonments in which they lived the privileged existence of an army of occupation. Sometimes these were existing cities like Damascus or Córdoba; more frequently they were new foundations such as Basra or Kufa (now Al Kūfah) in Mesopotamia, Fustat (Old Cairo) in Egypt or Kairouan in Tunisia. There is a symbolism in it all. One senses that they were not much interested in their subjects. People of the Book were useful, indispensable indeed, as taxpayers and administrators and artisans, but that was as far as it went. Their wider culture was not matter for investigation. Christians, on the other hand, could not be indifferent to Islam. The attitudes that we can document in this early period – misunderstanding, resentment, hostility – may with hindsight be lamentable but are all too intelligible given the circumstances and assumptions of the time. Aloofness on the one side and hostility on the other were to prove remarkably pervasive and enduring over the centuries which were to follow.

2

An Elephant for Charlemagne

In the year 750 a political coup took place in the governing circles of Islam. Abu-l-'Abbas, known as as-Saffah, 'the Shedder of Blood', liquidated the members of the ruling Umayyad dynasty and installed himself as caliph in Damascus. The new ruler claimed descent from the Prophet's uncle, al-'Abbas: hence his family is known as the Abbasid dynasty. His successor, al-Mansūr, moved the capital city of the Islamic empire to an entirely new, purpose-built capital at Baghdad in 762. There the Abbasids presided over the Islamic world until they were displaced by the Mongols in 1258. During the early Abbasid period Christendom and the *Dār al-Islām* became less intelligible to one another even as they continued to interact.

The Abbasid revolution was much more than a change of dynasty: it was a turning point in the history of Islam. The change of capitals was symbolic of much else. In Damascus the caliphs had taken over an already ancient city not far from the shores of the Mediterranean. Custodians of an inheritance which they could not wholeheartedly embrace, they superintended a successor-state composed of jumbled fragments of the two great empires of late antiquity but now run for the benefit of the Arab conquerors. Baghdad was different. It was in what is now Iraq; and the movement from the Mediterranean to Mesopotamia, several hundred miles to the east, signalled new orientations and horizons. It was in concept an exclusively Islamic city, carrying with it no distracting ragbag of earlier religious and cultural traditions. Its nucleus, the Round City built between 762 and 766, though in part derived from Persian models of town planning, was conceived as an architectural assertion of Islamic and Abbasid authority: at its heart there lay the elaborate complex of mosque and palace surrounded by an enormous acreage of gardens. Baghdad laid claim to a different form of legitimacy, announced a new style of rulership within the Islamic *umma*. Caliphal power, firmly located within the Abbasid family, became autocratic, exercised through a standing army and salaried officials. The ruler himself became remote and inaccessible, withdrawn from view behind a protective screen of courtly ritual. It was a style of government that owed something to the absolutist theocratic traditions of pre-Islamic Persia.

This is not wholly surprising, seeing that Persians were flocking into the ever-expanding bureaucracy housed in the new capital. They could rise to great heights. The most notable example in the early Abbasid period was the Barmakid family, originally from the far eastern frontiers of Iran and once Buddhist by faith, whose members formed the inner circle of government ministers under the caliph Hārūn ar-Rashīd (786–809). Buddhists no longer, however; they had become Muslims. This marks a contrast with the confessional allegiances of earlier officials such as the family of John of Damascus. Those had remained loyal to their religious traditions; later functionaries were more prone to transfer loyalties and embrace Islam. Why? We shall return

Santiago de
Compostela

FRANCIA

R. Danube

R. Dnieper

Venice

Black

Barcelona

Rome

Constantinople

Amalfi

Amorium

•Córdoba

SICILY

Tarsus
Antioch

CYPRUS

•Fez

MAGHRIB

Tripoli

Jerusalem

Alexandria

SINAI

R. Nile

| 0 | 800 km |
| 0 | 500 miles |

——— Approximate boundaries of Islamic dominion *c.*1000
——— Approximate boundaries of Eastern Roman/Byzantine Empire *c.*1000

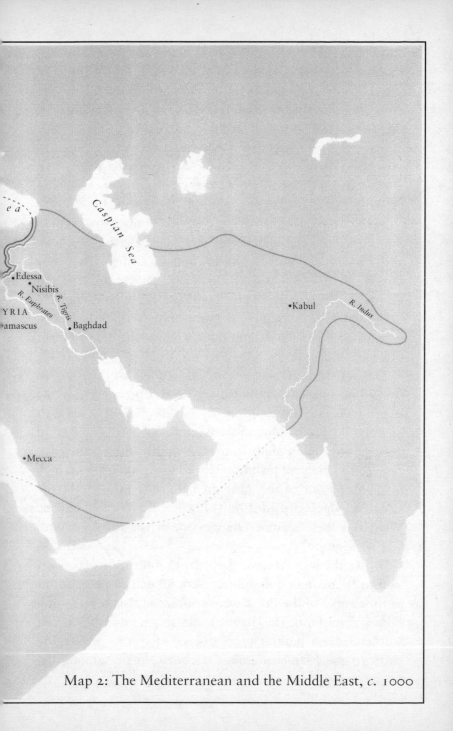

Map 2: The Mediterranean and the Middle East, *c.* 1000

to this question in a moment. For the present it is enough to say that a part of the answer is that they now found themselves more welcome in the Islamic fold. The Abbasids showed themselves more culturally inclusive than their predecessors.

One significant facet of this new openness was a willingness on the part of the elite to absorb the intellectual heritage of the ancient world. Just as Iraq lay at the centre of a commercial network which ranged throughout the entire Old World from the Atlantic to the Pacific, so too Islamic scholars could draw on the accumulated wisdom and expertise of Greek and Persian antiquity, of India and of China. This they did, in the early Abbasid period, with tremendous zest; and followed up this phase of absorption with a burst of intellectual creativity, especially in philosophy and the sciences, which had far-reaching consequences for the development of civilization.

This is to indicate some of the ways in which the Abbasid revolution opened new perspectives and prospects for the Islamic world. One could almost speak of a new sense of identity. Being a Muslim in the Baghdad of Hārūn ar-Rashīd must have been an almost unrecognizably different experience from being a Muslim in the conquering armies which first poured out of the Arabian Peninsula into the Fertile Crescent which girdled it only a century and a half earlier. What did these seismic changes mean for relations with Christendom?

During the early Abbasid period the momentum of conversion to Islam among its subject peoples gained pace. So far as the People of the Book were concerned, Islam was not a proselytizing faith. The Islamic leadership needed their taxes; so there was a built-in fiscal disincentive for encouraging entry to the Islamic *umma*. Of course, many among the subject peoples did make that leap. But into what? During the Umayyad period status, power and wealth remained the jealously guarded monopoly of the ethnically Arab Muslim elite. Converts to Islam had to be 'adopted' into an Arab clan as the *mawlā* or 'client' (plural *mawālī*) of a protector. The *mawālī* were not accorded the fullness of membership of the *umma* but remained second-class citizens still subject to a degree of discrimination (for example, financial). This caused resentment and social tension which finally became explosive. Disaffected *mawālī*, a numerous group by the second quarter of the eighth century, were among the strongest supporters of the Abbasid revolution. The coming of the Abbasids gave the *mawālī* what they wanted: equality of treatment in a society now defined by religion and culture rather than by ethnicity; an Islamic society rather than an Arab society.

Ethnically Arab in its ruling class it may no longer have been, but linguistically Arab it rapidly became. Arabic was the language of government and commerce as well as of faith; soon it would become the language of a rich and varied literature. Current from the Atlantic to Afghanistan, the Arabic language became one of the most potent unifying forces in the Abbasid Empire. Another such force was trade. The Abbasids presided over an enormous free-trade zone in which highly-prized goods such as precious textiles, incense, and culinary and cosmetic spices were regularly traded over very considerable distances on the backs of camels, donkeys or slaves – there was little wheeled traffic in medieval Islam. Merchants and craftsmen were respected people whose callings were valued and well regarded. The cities that grew up to sustain this commercial network shared certain common features – mosque and baths, souk, caravanserai and Koranic school – which helped the traveller to feel as at home in Fez as in Kabul. The blank walls of the houses which lined the narrow streets concealed the light and elegance which often lay within, focus for the warm family solidarity which was so distinctive a part of the moral culture of Islam. The schools taught knowledge of the Koran, the word of God made book, primarily by learning and oral recitation, but also by reading. This was a society which valued literacy and had a high regard for penmanship. To write a good clear hand was a prerequisite for employment in the burgeoning caliphal bureaucracy.

That is to suggest some of the salient features of the Islamic society that took shape under the rule of the Abbasids. The degree to which it was *confessionally* Islamic is a matter which scholars continue to debate. Shifts of religious allegiance are notoriously hard for historians to chart. They tend to be inadequately documented and resistant to explanation at any other than a superficial level. There is general agreement that a very large proportion of the indigenous populations in the lands conquered by Islamic armies did sooner or later relinquish Christianity, Judaism or Persian Zoroastrianism and adopt the Islamic faith of their conquerors. By the same token it is accepted that a minority, usually though not exclusively in the countryside rather than in inner cities or suburbs, retained their previous faith. The terms 'very large proportion' and 'minority' are regrettably but inescapably vague: we simply do not have the evidence on which to base a more precise assessment. With the warning that this is only a guess, we might hazard that somewhere between 75 per cent and 90 per cent of the indigenous non-rural populations in most parts of the Islamic world eventually became Muslims, somewhere between 10 per cent and 25 per cent did not.

'Eventually', because the rate of conversion seems to have been gradual. This is another area of uncertainty. Different methods for measuring the rate of conversion have been proposed. They range from the frankly impressionistic – such as by dating successive architectural extensions made to major city mosques in order to accommodate a growing number of believers – to the more disciplined statistical, as in the hands of the American scholar, Richard W. Bulliet, who has used changing patterns of name-giving as a guide to religious identity. A cautious consensus has emerged along these lines. During the first century or so of Islamic rule in any given region conversions seem to have been few and slow. Over the next couple of centuries or so there was a quickening of momentum, with many people throwing in their lot with the new faith. Thereafter the graph of conversion flattened out. In the present context of discussions about relations between Christianity and Islam, it will follow that in most of the central Islamic lands (Syria, Egypt, Iraq) conversion from Christianity to Islam was probably at its most intense between $c.750$ and $c.950$. In those areas conquered later, such as Spain, the time of greatest intensity would be correspondingly delayed to $c.800–1000$.

In important ways Christians assisted in the bringing to birth of an Islamic society: paradoxical but true. One of these has already been emphasized: the role of People of the Book as civil servants. The Islamic state depended on their efforts. They for their part found themselves little by little adopting features of Islamic culture – most obviously, the Arabic language – and becoming assimilated into its routines, customs, dress, diet and entertainments. Bit by bit such people, at any rate very many among them, would slip over the religious divide and embrace the faith as well as the culture of Islam.

Another way was by cooperation in introducing the Islamic elite to the intellectual culture of Hellenistic and Persian antiquity. The Christian communities of Syria and northern Mesopotamia were the main conduit. A first step was the translation of antique learning into the local Syriac vernacular. For example, George 'of the Arabians', a bishop in Mesopotamia who died in 724, translated a number of Aristotle's works into Syriac and composed commentaries upon them. The second step was the translation of this Syriac corpus into Arabic. It was one of the Barmakid family who commissioned the translation of Ptolemy's *Almagest* into Arabic, thus making available to Islamic scholars the most important work of astronomy produced in the ancient world. Or again, Ḥunayn ibn Isḥāq (d.873), an eastern Christian who was physician to the Abbasid caliph al-Mutawakkil, translated the medical works of Hippocrates and Galen from Syriac, and parts of the corpus also directly from Greek, into Arabic.

There was nothing planned about this transmission. It was occasioned simply by the desire of an Islamic ruling class which was now sedentary, wealthy and inquisitive to gain access to useful knowledge, and by the willingness of the Christian custodians of an intellectual tradition to make it available to new enquirers. In so far as there was any element of deliberation it was shaped by demand. The patrons and scholars of Islam were interested in practical wisdom, for example treatises on medicine, agriculture, botany or surveying, and in works that would assist them to a more exalted understanding of God's purposes, for instance astronomical books, or works of philosophy strictly so called such as those of the great 'Aflatun' or Plato. This quest had the sanction of the Prophet himself, who is alleged (among the Hadith or

'Traditions') to have said 'Seek knowledge, even unto China'. They were not interested in the literary, as opposed to the scientific or philosophical works of antiquity. The *Thousand and One Nights*, translated from Persian into Arabic in the ninth century, is perhaps the one exception which proves the rule. A few extracts from Homer were also translated from Greek into Arabic, but seem to have aroused little interest.

In the central Islamic lands of the Fertile Crescent, then, Christian and Muslim cooperated fruitfully in tilling the contiguous, often overlapping fields of professional service and intellectual exchange. Where they differed, they did so courteously. So much is suggested by an apologetic work written by a Christian convert to Islam. Al-Ṭabarī was a Christian bureaucrat who was drawn to the caliphal court, became a Muslim, composed some medical treatises and was the friend and adviser of the caliphs in the middle years of the ninth century. He wrote his religious tract to answer the objections of Christians to Islam. Identifying the prophethood of Muhammad as the central issue in contention, al-Ṭabarī addressed it with notable sensitivity to Christian feelings and defended it wherever possible with citations from Christian scripture. For example, scriptural references to prophets who postdated the life of Jesus (e.g. Acts 13:1) invalidated, argued al-Ṭabarī, some of the grounds for Christian rejection of the prophethood of Muhammad.

If you reflect on these proofs of prophecy and fulfilment, you will correctly find the reasons and causes for which we have accepted the Prophet Muhammad (peace be upon him), are the same reasons and causes by which you had accepted Christ and Moses (peace be upon them).[1]

One senses a background of good-mannered discussion between Muslim and Christian.

Christian Churches under Islamic rule – Monophysite (or Coptic), Syriac, and other sects – have often been referred to as 'captive' Churches. No label could be more misleading. Released from the bondage of Constantinopolitan persecution they flourished as never before, generating in the process a rich spiritual literature in hymns, prayers, sermons and devotional works. Not all branches of the Christian Church blossomed so extravagantly under an Islamic dispensation. Others experienced isolation. The Churches of Nubia in the upper reaches of the Nile, and of Ethiopia still further south, managed to maintain intermittent contact with their mother-churches, notably Alexandria. As time went by, however, this proved more and more difficult. The Nubian Church would eventually fizzle out, though it was a long time a-dying. In Ethiopia, by contrast, the Church throve in isolation, developing along markedly individual lines. When Portuguese visitors entered the country in the early sixteenth century it would be a very peculiar Christian society which they found there, distinctive in its Hebraic practices (circumcision, dietary prescriptions, reverence for the Ark of the Covenant) and in a monastic life very different from that of contemporary Europe.

In North Africa to the west of Egypt Christianity fared less well. It has always puzzled historians that the Church whose vitality can be felt in the writings of early Christian fathers such as Tertullian, Cyprian and Augustine should have faded as it did under Islam. A part of the answer may be that the process of Islamic conquest was longer and much more disruptive in North Africa than it had been in Egypt or Syria. This encouraged emigration by leading figures in the African

Church to nearby havens in Italy or southern France where they could be sure of a welcome. (It will be remembered that emigration was not an option for the 'heretics' of the eastern Churches such as John of Damascus: they had to stay put and flourish where they were, because for them the Empire of East Rome was no haven.) Emigration took some to distant and unexpected destinations. An African monk named Hadrian was plucked from a haven near Naples and sent off to be the abbot of a community at Canterbury. The school over which he presided there for some forty years did much valuable work in introducing the young English Church to the learning of Mediterranean Christendom.

Another part of the answer may be that North Africa had less to offer Islam than Middle Eastern Christianity. Carthage simply did not possess the intellectual resources of Alexandria, Edessa or Nisibis. And indeed on the Muslim side there was probably a good deal less local interest in, or receptivity to, such resources. In the eighth and ninth centuries the Maghrib and Spain were the Wild West of the Muslim world, turbulent borderlands unconducive to intellectual cultivation.

The luxury of reasonably peaceful coexistence enjoyed by such as Ḥunayn ibn Isḥāq and his master the caliph would have been incomprehensible and unpalatable, had they known about it, to the ruling classes of Christendom proper, that is the area under Christian secular rule in what was left of the Roman Empire and in the Germanic kingdoms of Western Europe. To these people Islam presented itself primarily as a military threat. The East Roman, or as we may now begin to call it the Byzantine Empire, experienced its gravest peril between about 650 and 850, symbolized by the two bruising sieges of Constantinople in 674–78 and

716–18. The walls of the imperial city saved the Empire on those two occasions. On others it owed its survival, variously, to the mountain barriers of Cilicia (in today's eastern Turkey), to dogged professional resistance by land and sea, to an inherited infrastructure of effective taxation, and to the confidence born of a sense of Romano-Christian identity fostered by the Church. The removal of the seat of the caliphs from Damascus to Baghdad signalled a turning eastward on the part of the ruling circles of Islam. No longer facing out over the Mediterranean, their resolve to shatter the Empire began to show signs of weakening. But it was to be a long time before security returned. As late as 838 Islamic armies invaded Asia Minor: the Emperor Theophilus lost a battle and very nearly his life; the important city of Amorion was sacked; hordes of prisoners were taken back to Syria, the grander to await ransom, the rank and file into lifelong slavery. Not until the second half of the ninth century could the Byzantine Empire, by then no longer a superpower, begin to feel safe. Not until the tenth did she go once more on the offensive, in an East Roman *reconquista* under soldier-emperors like Nicephorus Phocas and John Tzimisces that would bring Christian rule back to such places as Tarsus, Cyprus and Antioch.

The outlook was as gloomy in the central Mediterranean. The Islamic conquest of Sicily began in 827. Rome was raided in 846. For a generation between 843 and 871 the Muslims had a toehold on the mainland, at Bari in Apulia, whence they could launch raids on the Adriatic coasts of Italy and Dalmatia. Ousted from Bari, they soon acquired another mainland base on the western coast near Naples, which they held until 915. Once the Muslim grip on Sicily was secure, the maritime regions of Calabria were repeatedly attacked. The assaults on Italy were the work of freelance pirates, opportunists who were out for what they could get, not operations directed by the state, and with hindsight we can see that it was unlikely that any permanent Islamic presence on the mainland would strike root. But such comforting reflections were not available to contemporaries who were as thoroughly demoralized by these sea-borne predators as were their northern fellow Christians by the Vikings. To resist these enemies was surely to do God's work. Pope Leo IV, appealing for help against the Saracens in 853, said as much: whoever lost his life in this conflict would go to heaven.

The sole survivor of as-Saffāh's bloody annihilation of the Umayyad family had made his way hazardously to Spain – invariably styled 'al-Andalus' in Arabic sources* – where he had set up an independent Islamic principality based at Córdoba which his descendants ruled until the eleventh century. They kept up a fairly constant pressure on their Christian neighbours: the rump of the Visigothic kingdom which had taken refuge in the north-west, and in the north-east the southern marchlands of the Frankish Empire of Charlemagne in Catalonia. At times the pressure became intense. Towards the end of the tenth century one ruler of al-Andalus was credited with fifty-seven campaigns against the Christians in twenty-one years. These included an attack on one of western Christendom's most sacred shrines,

---

* The name al-Andalus has long puzzled historians and philologists. Derivation from an Arabic phrase, perhaps Berber-descended, meaning 'land of the Vandals' seems likely. The Vandals were Germanic invaders of the Western Roman Empire who passed through Spain in the early fifth century and ended up ruling a sub-Roman kingdom in North Africa.

the tomb of the apostle St James at Santiago de Compostela, in 997.

Neither was southern Gaul spared. At La Garde-Freinet, between Toulon and Cannes, just inland from St Tropez, a nest of pirates was established towards the end of the ninth century which lasted for some eighty years. Their depredations took in coastal shipping, the Alpine valleys and the basin of the Rhône. Their most distinguished prize was Abbot Mayeul of the great Burgundian monastery of Cluny, captured as he was traversing the Alps on his homeward way from Rome. His captors demanded a thousand pounds weight of silver for his release; and got it too, after the monks of Cluny had melted down all their church plate. The pirates of La Garde-Freinet were not finally smoked out until 972.

Throughout the Mediterranean world, therefore, Christendom was on the defensive. The threat was not simply a military one, whether represented by caliphal armies in Turkey or unruly kidnappers in Provence. It was during this same epoch, as we have seen, that the tempo of conversion to Islam was quickening. Christian leaders could watch their congregations dwindling from Sunday to Sunday; always an uncomfortable experience. By chance we possess testimony to the anxieties of two Christian communities at opposite ends of the Mediterranean in the middle years of the ninth century. The first concerns the so-called Mozarabic Christians of southern Spain, 'Mozarab' being the name – derived from an Arabic word meaning 'Arabized' – applied to the Christians who lived under Islamic rule in Spain. During the 850s a number of Christians in Córdoba, seat of Umayyad authority in al-Andalus, and smaller numbers elsewhere, deliberately and publicly insulted Islam and so brought upon themselves the capital punishment which the sharia, the religious law of Islam, prescribes for this offence. Reactions to their deaths divided the Christian communities in al-Andalus. In some quarters they were hailed as martyrs; in others their sufferings were regarded as spurious martyrdoms because they had sought death voluntarily. Works in their defence were composed and have come down to us. They cast welcome shafts of light upon the mood of the Mozarabic communities. The priest Eulogius, himself to suffer martyrdom in 859, and his friend Paul Alvar, the authors of these works, evidently belonged to a more intense or 'committed' tendency among the Christians which was worried by the leaching away of Christian youth towards Islamic faith and culture. The incidental information which they provide about the worlds of family and work summons up a credible context of rather fluid religious allegiances in which all sorts of humdrum pressures were impelling Christians towards Islam.

Take the young man named Isaac, the earliest victim to be executed in Córdoba, in 851. Isaac belonged to a well-to-do Christian family in the city. He had been well educated and was a fluent Arabic speaker. His skills secured him a posting in the civil service where he quickly rose to high rank. At that point he experienced a religious vocation, resigned his employment and became a monk in a nearby monastery. There he came to feel that it was his duty to witness to his faith by defying Islam. He sought an audience with the *qāḍi*, or religious judge, of Córdoba, ostensibly for the purpose of receiving instruction in the faith of Islam. In the present context what is of interest is that the *qāḍi* assumed that this was a routine matter: evidently such requests were frequent. In the event Isaac violently denounced Islam, and suffered the penalty that Islamic law lays down for this offence. Or take the case of the two sisters Alodia and Nunilo, natives not of Córdoba but of the northern town of Huesca in the foothills of the Pyrenees. They were the children of a mixed marriage between a Muslim man and a Christian woman. The father had permitted the mother to bring the girls up as Christians. After his death the mother remarried, once more to a Muslim. The second husband proved less accommodating, and his wife sent her daughters to stay with her Christian sister so that they would be out of harm's way and their faith would not be under threat. However, a neighbour who was an enemy of the family denounced the sisters to the authorities as apostates from Islam. Arrested, they were promised all sorts of inducements, such as help in arranging advantageous marriages, if they would renounce Christianity. This they refused to do, and in consequence were publicly beheaded.

These humdrum pressures to follow Islam, then, might be those of neighbourhood, marriage, the need for patronage or employment, the peer pressure of youth. These are forces for conversion which are familiar in all sorts of other historical contexts. Conformity with an establishment is comfortable and advantageous. Worldly this may be, but all too human. The zealots were outraged at it. They felt themselves and their Christian culture, their identity, threatened. At one community in particular, the monastery of Tabanos just outside Córdoba, feelings of anxiety and outrage seem to have been stoked up to a hot intensity. Eventually the explosive mixture boiled over. It was from Tabanos that many of the martyrs emerged, chosen by God, as they tragically believed, to bear witness for their faith before a world that was betraying it and them.

At about the same time as these events in Spain, an anonymous monk in a Palestinian monastery was composing, in Arabic, a work in defence of Christianity. The enemies whom he specifically identified in his opening chapter were people in the Christian community of his own day whom he regarded as dissemblers.

They hide their faith, and they divulge to them [i.e. Muslims] what suits them . . . They stray off the road which leads to the kingdom of heaven . . . hypocrites among us, marked with our mark, standing in our congregations, contradicting our faith, forfeiters of themselves, who are Christians in name only.[2]

The confessional situation envisaged was evidently similar to that assumed in the writings of Eulogius and Paul Alvar. In Palestine as in Spain, Christianity was being weakened by desertion, diluted by hypocrisy. And the Christians of the two regions knew about each other. A monk of St Saba – once home to John of Damascus – named George paid a visit to southern Spain. We hear about him only because he joined the zealots and with them was executed in 852. It follows that there could have been others like him of whom we know nothing. Anxious Christians could share their worries, compare notes, discuss possible courses of action.

It is easy enough to understand how a monastic environment, whether at St Saba or at Tabanos, might foster a specially intense religious zeal. Christians who lived in the world outside, however, might find that prudent accommodation was advisable – even though purists might condemn this as betrayal. This would seem to have been the attitude of the senior Mozarabic bishop in al-Andalus, Reccafred of Seville, who immediately condemned the 'martyrs' of

Córdoba as false, because voluntary. It was to counter such critics that Eulogius and Paul Alvar composed their polemical works. Nice questions of defining genuine martyrdom apart, zealots could accuse Reccafred and his like of being Arabizers, collaborators with Islamic authority. We do not possess Reccafred's answer to such accusations, but he could plausibly have claimed that by being accommodating he was acting in the best interests of his flock, deflecting possible persecution. There are hard and perennial moral questions to be pondered here.

A century after the martyrdoms in Córdoba the same dilemmas were present. In the middle years of the tenth century several embassies were exchanged between the court of Otto I of Germany and that of Córdoba. (The purpose of these diplomatic exchanges may have been to organize joint action against the pirates of La Garde-Freinet; with what success we do not know.) One of these, in 953, was led by a prominent German monk, John, from the Rhineland abbey of Gorze. At his destination he met another Christian named John, a bishop, presumably of Córdoba. This Spanish bishop explained to his visitor how the Christians of al-Andalus managed to survive:

Consider under what conditions we live. We have been driven to this by our sins, to be subjected to the rule of the pagans. We are forbidden by the Apostle's words to resist the civil power. Only one cause of solace is left to us, that in the depths of such a great calamity they do not forbid us to practise our own faith ... For the time being, then, we keep the following counsel: that provided no harm is done to our religion, we obey them in all else, and do their commands in all that does not affect our faith.[3]

John of Gorze was shocked at what he saw as cowardice and was all for confrontation:

Somewhat angered, John of Gorze replied: 'It would be fitting for someone other than you, a bishop, to utter such sentiments. Your superior rank should have made you a defender of the faith . . . Never could I approve that the divine laws should be transgressed out of fear or for friendship . . . Even if I accept that you, constrained by necessity, fall in line with them, I, by the grace of God free from such necessity, will in no way be deflected by any fear or enticement or favour . . . I will not for the sake of life itself run away from the task of witnessing to the truth.'[4]

Fortunately for himself he was persuaded to desist from this fiery stance and his embassy, not without further ups and downs, eventually passed off satisfactorily. Our authority for this is John of Gorze's biographer, writing shortly after his death with the aim of publicizing his abbot's claims to sanctity. We should not expect a hagiographer to minimize his subject's Christian heroism. In other words, the reported encounter between the two Johns may not be literally true in every detail. But the general context is surely convincing. The Mozarabic Christians of al-Andalus were a cowed and rather timid band. Let us remember that a century of steadily-advancing conversion to Islam had elapsed since the time of Eulogius. Visitors from trans-Pyrenean Christendom were punchy and confrontational, and praised for this by their fellow Christians at home: something of a portent.

Western Christendom had developed in the early medieval period along completely different lines from the emergent society of Islam under the Abbasids. Where the *Dār al-Islām* was a world of cities linked by regular commerce, the West was overwhelmingly agrarian in its economy. Towns were small and thinly scattered, trade for the most part (but not exclusively, as we shall see soon) local and small-scale. The merchant was not a figure of weight or status in society. The infrastructure of what had once been Roman order – a unified legal system, taxation, bureaucracy, a standing army – had withered obscurely away. The Frankish state under Charlemagne (768–814) was both extensive and powerful; but in comparison to the Abbasid Empire governed by his contemporary Hārūn ar-Rashīd it was as a minnow to a whale. And it worked in an altogether different way. Royal power rested ultimately upon the loyalty and cooperation of an unruly military aristocracy whose great landed families lorded it over their regions with a minimum of what we should recognize as government. Literacy did not extend much beyond the clergy (and even among them was minimal at lower levels): reading and writing were not skills highly regarded as they were in the Islamic world. The scientific and philosophical learning of classical antiquity had been almost entirely forgotten, as indeed had the Greek language in which it had been transmitted. It had been replaced by an intellectual culture based principally upon the Bible and the Latin Fathers of the Church such as St Augustine, a culture inturned, backward-looking and deeply conservative. It is no wonder that Muslims of the Abbasid age evinced so little interest in western or Latin Christendom: it had nothing obvious to offer them. The dismissive attitude of a tenth-century traveller and geographer, Ibn Ḥawqal, was typical: Francia, he recorded, was a good source of slaves; that was all there was to be said about it.

That does not mean that there were no interactions

between Christendom and the *Dār al-Islām*. On the contrary, such interactions were both more intense and more diverse than they had been in the previous Umayyad era. There were diplomatic relations, for a start. Charlemagne and Hārūn ar-Rashīd were in diplomatic contact round about the year 800 – a significant year, in which Charlemagne was crowned Emperor in Rome on Christmas Day. The caliph's presentation to the Frankish ruler of an elephant named Abu-l-'Abbas (after the founder of his dynasty), which arrived in Italy via Tunisia in the year 801, may just possibly have been connected with this development, seeing that elephants had for many centuries been a symbol of authority in the near east. The exotic creature formed a tenuous link between two cultures which could hardly have been more disparate. Abu-l-'Abbas plodded majestically to – presumably – Charlemagne's principal residence at Aachen in the Rhineland where he survived for nine, probably uncomfortable, years: a sufficiently important personage for his death to be noted in the official royal annals for the year 810.

Negotiations for the freeing of prisoners of war was a frequent occasion for diplomatic exchanges. Early in the tenth century, for example, St Demetrianus of Cyprus was despatched to Baghdad on a mission of this nature, with covering letters from the patriarch of Constantinople, Nicholas Mysticos, to 'the best of my friends',[5] the Abbasid caliph. This is the language of diplomacy. Officials in Constantinople kept records of diplomatic exchanges and files devoted to neighbouring peoples and how to deal with them. The seventh-century lapses in intelligence-gathering were not to be repeated. A tenth-century handbook of selections from such documents made under the direction of the scholarly emperor, Constantine Porphyrogenitus, has survived, a tantalizing glimpse of what the lost imperial archives once contained.

When St Demetrianus was sent to Baghdad his homeland of Cyprus had been under Islamic rule for some two and a half centuries. Presumably Demetrianus was fluent in Arabic, to qualify him for his mission. In the same way Islamic authorities employed Christian churchmen with a knowledge of Latin on missions to Christian rulers. John of Gorze's embassy to al-Andalus was reciprocated by the sending of a cleric named Recemund from Córdoba to the court of Otto I of Germany. Recemund was Mozarabic bishop of Elvira (the later Granada) in southern Spain, and an important figure in the intellectual life of al-Andalus.

Travel was easy in the linguistically and culturally unified world of Islam under the Abbasids. A man like Ibn Ḥawqal travelled very widely, both within the *Dār al-Islām* and beyond it. His journeyings even took him on the perilous overland crossing of the Sahara, right down south to the Niger Valley where gold came from. Yet travellers such as he never ventured into Christendom. (Businessmen sometimes did, as we shall see.) They were simply not interested in what they might find there. In many ways the world of Islam in the Abbasid period was self-contained. Muslim holy places, for example, lay within the *Dār al-Islām*: the pilgrim to Mecca did not have to leave it. For Christians, on the other hand, the holiest of places now lay outside Christendom. Throughout these centuries a steady trickle of pilgrims made their way to Jerusalem and the other holy sites of Palestine. Some of them, a very few, have left accounts of their travels which have come down to us. These itineraries usually concern themselves simply with sacred topography. Just occasionally, however, they contain reactions to the contemporary world encountered by the pilgrims. A Frankish bishop named Arculf was one of the earliest. He visited the eastern Mediterranean lands in the 670s. While in Egypt he watched crocodiles in the Nile, and in recording how he tried to walk across Alexandria in a single day vividly conveys the enormous size of that city. No carts, so familiar a sight in his native Gaul, were to be seen in Palestine: camels did all the carrying. In Damascus 'the unbelieving Saracens' had built themselves 'a new church',[6] which we know as the great Umayyad mosque. Arculf's ship was blown off course on his way home somewhere off the Atlantic coast of Gaul and he ended up after various adventures in the monastery of Iona off the west coast of Scotland. It was while staying at Iona that he dictated the account of his pilgrimage to a monastic scribe. What is notable in this and other accounts is the lack of interest evinced in Islamic religious culture. In general, Christians were no more interested in Islam than Muslims were in Christianity.

This was not the sort of interaction which underlay the process of cultural diffusion. Christian artists and craftsmen could work on early Islamic religious buildings such as the mosque which Arculf saw in Damascus or the Dome of the Rock in Jerusalem, instructing their new masters in the techniques of the stone-carver and mosaicist. A twelfth-century writer recorded the tradition that the caliph al-Walīd I (705–15) had asked the emperor in Constantinople to send him 12,000 craftsmen to work on the mosque of Damascus: the number may be exaggerated, but the underlying story is credible. Other practical techniques passed to and fro, though we can rarely spot the technicians. Take the case of the dreaded 'Greek fire', or as Constantine Porphyrogenitus termed it 'the liquid fire which is discharged through tubes'

– it was probably petroleum-based – the secret of which, he claimed, had been revealed by God through an angel to Constantine the Great, with strict instructions that 'it should be manufactured among the Christians only and in the City ruled by them [i.e. Constantinople], and nowhere else at all; nor should it be sent nor taught to any other nation whatsoever'.[7] A more prosaic story held that it was invented by a seventh-century engineer from the Lebanon named Callinicus who fled from Islam into the Byzantine empire bringing his formula with him. If the authorities did try to keep the recipe secret, they were not successful for long. By the time that Constantine Porphyrogenitus was committing his information to writing – complete with a moral story about the appropriate fate of an official who was bribed to release the secret (consumed by fire from heaven) – Islamic naval commanders had long been familiar with these pyrotechnics. Greek fire had become 'a standard part of a warship's armoury'[8] by the tenth century for Christian and Muslim alike.

A humbler example of diffusion from Christendom to the *Dār al-Islām* is furnished by the cork-soled sandal. This was a form of footwear developed in the Roman period in Spain, employing the bark of the cork-oak. (The English word 'cork' is probably derived indirectly from Latin *quercus*, 'oak'.) After the Muslim conquest of Spain the fashion for this lightweight, durable, comfortable and inexpensive footwear was taken up by the conquerors and spread eastwards by way of north Africa to the central Islamic heartlands. Fourteen centuries later it is still with us.

From manifold examples of transmission of techniques in the other direction, from the *Dār al-Islām* to Christendom, we may cite three, simple but of critical importance. One is the technique of raising water for the purposes of irrigation by an animal-powered machine called in Arabic a *saqiya*. The animal – donkey, mule or camel – is tethered to a draw-bar which turns a wheel. By a simple piece of gearing this wheel in turn rotates another wheel which is vertically set over the source of the water. This vertical wheel has pots slung onto its circumference which fill as it goes round, discharging their contents at the turn of the wheel into a holding tank whence the water can be distributed. Construction and maintenance are not complicated; the saving in human labour is prodigious. The *saqiya* was known in the eastern Mediterranean lands in the pre-Islamic period, but its really wide diffusion occurred under Islam. Probably known in Spain by the ninth century, the *saqiya* was discussed by Andalusian agronomical writers of the eleventh century, who recommended that hardwoods such as olive be used for the vertical ('pot-garland') wheel and that the pots be provided with a vent to prevent breakage caused by the force of the water. A twelfth-century Andalusian poet even celebrated waterwheels in verse. The Christians of Spain adopted this technology from their Muslim neighbours or took it over when they reconquered Muslim territory. Much of the vocabulary of hydraulics in modern Spanish is derived from Arabic.

A second example is the abacus. This simple piece of technology for aiding mathematical calculation had been known throughout the ancient world from the Roman Empire to China. Knowledge of it had disappeared from the early medieval West. Its reintroduction can, most unusually, be reliably dated and attributed. In the 960s a young French cleric named Gerbert of Aurillac spent some time studying in Catalonia. Returning to France he settled at Rheims for some years where he acquired celebrity as a teacher of mathematics. Writing to a friend in 984 he asked to borrow 'a little book *On the Multiplication and Division of Numbers* by Joseph the Spaniard'.[9] The term *Hispanus*, 'the Spaniard', indicated at that date a recent immigrant from al-Andalus, Muslim Spain, not just any inhabitant of the Iberian Peninsula. Joseph the Spaniard was therefore a Christian or Jewish immigrant from the Muslim south who brought his learning with him and whose mathematical treatise had come to Gerbert's notice while he was studying in Catalonia. Gerbert himself wrote a textbook on the abacus which was almost certainly based on the lost work of Joseph. During the eleventh century knowledge of the abacus was diffused in western Christendom, rendering rapid and exact calculation feasible there for the first time. When Abbot Odilo of Cluny – successor to Mayeul who was captured at La Garde-Freinet – was on his deathbed in 1049 he wanted to know how many masses he had celebrated in his long abbacy of fifty-five years: the monastery's abacist was on hand to work it out.

A third and final example is paper. Islamic sources claim that the secrets of paper-making were wrung from Chinese prisoners-of-war captured at Samarkand after a battle early in the Abbasid period. Whether or not this story is true, it is certain that paper was being produced in Baghdad before the end of the eighth century, and that the spread of the technology from there to Syria, Egypt and North Africa can be traced over the succeeding two centuries or so. Among the various grades of paper listed by an encyclopedist of technology was a special lightweight type known as 'birds' paper' because it was thin enough to be sent by carrier pigeon: the earliest known airmail paper. In al-Andalus the town of

Játiva, near Valencia, became the most important centre for the manufacture of paper. Knowledge of the technique spread to Christian Spain. Paper was being produced in Catalonia by the twelfth century (at the latest). In 1196 witnesses in Barcelona could declare without surprise that the will of a lately-deceased civil servant had been copied, presumably with other personal documentation, into 'a certain paper book (*libro de paperio*)'.[10] After King James I of Aragon conquered Játiva in 1244 the paper-making industry there continued under royal protection, enabling the royal chancery to go over from parchment to paper as its principal writing material.

These techniques, and many others, were encountered by the Arabs in the course of their conquests, adopted and diffused within the Islamic world, and subsequently exported to Christendom. The same pattern of diffusion holds good for the book-learning of antiquity. As we saw earlier in this chapter, the transmission of learning from Greek via Syriac into Arabic was going forward at a brisk pace during the eighth and ninth centuries. Two linked processes then occurred. One was the extension and elaboration of this corpus of knowledge by the learned men of Islam. The other was its spread throughout the *Dār al-Islām*.

Three names may be chosen from many to illustrate the phase of expansion and elaboration. Al-Kindī (*c.*800–867) was the first major philosopher to emerge in the Islamic world. A high-ranking civil servant in Baghdad and adviser to the caliphal family, he wrote on a whole range of subjects – among much else mathematics, astronomy, astrology, chemistry, metallurgy and dreams. As a thinker, however, his main claim to fame is as the earliest within Islam to ponder the question of the relationship between Greek, specifically

Aristotelian, philosophy, and revelation as embodied in the Koran; and to attempt their partial harmonization.

Ibn Sīnā, known in the West as Avicenna (980–1037), was another habitué of courts and adviser of princes, though he lived in more troubled times than Al-Kindī and his career was fairly turbulent. As a philosopher he was attracted to these same perennial problems of the conflicting claims of reason and revelation. His major work the *Kitāb ash-Shifā*, 'the Book of the Cure [of Ignorance]', was a kind of encyclopedia of philosophy organized under the headings of Logic, Physics, Mathematics and Metaphysics, drawing extensively upon Plato, Aristotle and the Neoplatonists. Ibn Sīnā was equally distinguished as a physician, working out from the medical treatises of antiquity as summed up in the writings of Galen. His *al-Qānūn* [Canon of Medicine] remained a standard medical textbook for centuries after his death.

His close contemporary al-Bīrūnī (973–1048) was a man of formidable scientific learning and skills. In his capacity as a princely adviser he travelled in India where he learned Sanskrit. This enabled him to play a significant role in familiarizing his fellow Muslims with the learning of Hinduism, particularly through the medium of his encyclopedic *Kitāb al-Hind* [Book of India]. He produced in addition works on such topics as astronomy, botany and pharmacology. It is a measure of the degree to which Islamic men of science surpassed their predecessors that he described roughly five times as many medicinal plants as had Dioscorides, the greatest pharmacologist of antiquity, a thousand years beforehand. A skilled maker of scientific instruments, al-Bīrūnī took sightings in 1018 near modern Islamabad on which he based calculations of the radius and circumference of the earth which were astonishingly accurate, respectively 15 and 200 kilometres adrift from today's estimates.

Cultural diffusion within the Islamic world is once more appositely illustrated by the reception of Middle Eastern learning in the far west, which was rapidly shedding its earlier character of wildness. Fez, founded early in the ninth century, quickly acquired a reputation for learning, as did Córdoba under its Umayyad rulers in the tenth. One of the latter, indeed, was a noted bibliophile whose purchasers ranged as far afield as Iran and who maintained a team of calligraphers in Córdoba for the rapid multiplication of books acquired. Princely patronage was always one of the most significant factors in cultural diffusion. The outside agency of diplomatic exchange could also be a factor. A Byzantine embassy in 949 presented to the court of Córdoba a luxury copy of the works of Dioscorides. Dioscorides had already been translated into Arabic, but the translation had evidently not yet made its way to al-Andalus. There were no scholars in Spain who knew Greek, so an appeal was sent back to Constantinople in answer to which a learned Greek monk named Nicholas was sent to Spain in 951. A Muslim scholar from Sicily with a knowledge of Greek was also found. Together these two expounded the text to a group of Spanish scholars. This group was a most interesting one. It included native Andalusian Islamic scholars such as Ibn Juljul, who later composed a commentary on Dioscorides; a distinguished Jewish physician and courtier, Hasday ibn Shaprut; and the Mozarabic bishop Recemund of Elvira (he who was sent on an embassy to Germany), who was himself the author of the so-called *Calendar of Córdoba*, a work containing much agronomical and botanical information. It was a truly international and interdenominational gathering of scholars.

From their studies and discussions there sprouted an informal 'school' of scientific botanists active in eleventh-century Spain, often professionally attached to the gardens so prized by the elite of the Islamic world, gardens which had important functions as physic gardens in addition to their primary role as places of relaxation, delight to the senses and foretaste of the Gardens of Paradise.

Diplomacy, pilgrimage, techniques, ideas: to these varied occasions of interaction between Christendom and the Islamic world we must add one more: trade. Study of early medieval trade is inseparably connected with the name of the great Belgian historian Henri Pirenne (1862–1935). Contemplating the transition from the Roman to the medieval world order, Pirenne accorded central significance to the economic effects of the coming of Islam. His ideas were initially expounded in the unlikely surroundings of an internment camp to which he had been consigned in 1916 by the German occupying forces in Belgium. There he delivered a course of lectures on European economic history for his fellow internees, lectures in which were embedded the seeds of the celebrated 'Pirenne thesis'. Developed after the First World War in a number of articles and books published in the 1920s, Pirenne's ideas received their final articulation in a book which he completed shortly before his death. An English translation of it was published in 1939 under the title *Mohammed and Charlemagne*. Pirenne's central contention was at heart a simple one. Roman order had rested upon an infrastructure of cities and commerce in the Mediterranean which was little if at all disrupted by the Germanic invasions of the fifth century. Dislocation and change came later, in the seventh, and their agent was Islam. By taking over the Mediterranean and excluding others from participation in its economic life the Muslims drove western Christendom back upon itself. Denied access to the urbanized economy of the south, a Western European culture typified by the kingdom of the Franks took shape which was 'undeveloped', rural and feudal. In his most famous aphorism Pirenne put it thus: 'It is therefore strictly correct to say that without Mohammed Charlemagne would have been inconceivable.'[11]

The Pirenne thesis has been widely debated among historians for some eighty years. There is a kind of massive and incontrovertible truth about it. The eruption of Islam into the Mediterranean world *did* slice it in half, *did* reduce the Eastern Roman Empire to a shadow of its former self, *did* create the conditions in which a north-westerly migration of Christian culture could lead on to the flourishing of a civilization grouped about the shores of the northern seas. All this is incontestable. As against this, however, much of the detail of Pirenne's argument now looks unconvincing. Disciplines such as medieval archaeology and numismatics, which were in their infancy in Pirenne's day, have vastly enlarged the data available. Archaeological evidence, for example from the city of Marseilles, now suggests that severe economic dislocation was starting to occur in the Mediterranean world well *before* the coming of Islam on to the scene. More attentive scrutiny of the written sources has made historians wary of drawing from them the conclusions which Pirenne drew. His use of material derived from hagiographical texts, for instance, now appears crudely mechanistic in the light of the subtleties of purpose and structure revealed by recent study of these works. Pirenne's own assumptions and preoccupations may have misled him. A member of the *haute bourgeoisie* which had prospered from Belgium's industrial revolution, Pirenne had no interest whatsoever in agriculture and rural society, a temperamental handicap which led to misapprehensions about the economic life of the overwhelmingly agrarian societies of the ancient and early medieval worlds. In a word, the economic and social history of the European early Middle Ages now appears more complicated and nuanced and diverse than the grand simplicities proposed by Pirenne.

Middle Eastern Islam exerted a pull upon its neighbours by reason of its insatiable demand for certain commodities. The mushroom growth of Baghdad – probably the most rapidly growing city that the world had ever seen – and the ensuing foundation of further palace-cities, such as Samarra on the Tigris, required armies of slaves for construction work and domestic service. Slaves were sought wherever they might be found, in East Africa, Central Asia and the northern wilderness that later became Russia. In this latter region the principal suppliers were Scandinavian merchant adventurers referred to in our sources as *Rus* or *Rhos*. A Muslim official named Ibn Faḍlān has left a vivid record of these people, whom he encountered in the course of a diplomatic mission to a Turkic chieftain on the upper Volga in 922.

When they have come from their land and anchored on, or tied up at the shore of, the Volga, which is a great river, they build big houses of wood on the shore, each holding ten to twenty persons more or less ... When the ships come to this mooring place, everybody goes ashore with bread, meat, onions, milk and beer and betakes himself to a long upright piece of wood that has a face like a man's and is surrounded by little figures, behind which are long stakes in the ground. The Rus prostrates himself before the big carving and says, 'Oh my Lord, I have come from a far land

and have with me such and such a number of girls and such and such a number of sable-furs', and he proceeds to enumerate all his other wares. Then he says, 'I have brought you these gifts,' and lays down what he has brought with him, and continues, 'I wish that you would send me a merchant with many dinars and dirhems, who will buy from me whatever I wish.'[12]

Slaves would swell the labour force of Islam, exotic furs would mark out its ruling classes in the cold Iranian winters. They would be paid for in the silver coin, the dinars and dirhems, of Abbasid Islam. Thousands and thousands of such coins have been found deposited in Russian and Scandinavian coin hoards, incontrovertible numismatic testimony to the accuracy of Ibn Faḍlān's report. Some of this wealth of silver bullion, flowing most abundantly northwards in the ninth and tenth centuries, would be invested in other enterprises, notably trading with the peoples of Western Europe. It is no coincidence that the most marked urban growth to occur in the West since the Roman period took place at the centres to which Scandinavian traders resorted and in which they settled: Rouen, Lincoln, York, Dublin. In such an indirect fashion did the economic pull of Middle Eastern Islam foster the growth of a Western European bourgeoisie. As far as northern Europe is concerned, Pirenne's thesis has to be turned upside down.

Pirenne's judgement that the Mediterranean became an Islamic lake from which Christian merchants were excluded was certainly an exaggeration. The pre-Islamic economic dislocation referred to above possibly owed its origin – the matter remains under discussion – to demographic decline caused by plague. Long-distance trade in the Mediterranean fell off, towns contracted, industries decayed.

Even Constantinople itself suffered, with public buildings neglected and large spaces within its fifth-century walls given over to market-gardening and the grazing of sheep and goats. Recession was prolonged, its trough occurring in the eighth century and an almost imperceptibly slow up-turn beginning in the ninth. Yet commercial contact between Christian and Muslim lands never wholly ceased. The papal chancery continued to produce documents written on papyrus imported from Egypt throughout this period. King Alfred the Great of the English kingdom of Wessex (871–99) gave his biographer and friend, the Welsh priest Asser, 'a strong man's load of incense'[13] which must have originated in East Africa or India, presumably imported to western Christendom by way of the Mediterranean.

By the time that we get to the tenth and eleventh centuries there seem to have been fairly lively commercial interchanges between Christian and Muslim businessmen. Two Italian towns, in particular, were significant channels for the inflow of goods from the Islamic world: Amalfi to the south of Naples and, in the north-east, Venice. The Amalfitans had prospered by making the best of a bad job and siding with the Muslim raiders of the tenth century; their reward came in the form of commercial privileges. Amalfi's merchants made fortunes by importing the luxury commodities that the feudal aristocracy of Western Europe clamoured for – silk textiles, all manner of spices, ivory. No wonder that Ibn Ḥawqal considered it 'the most prosperous town in Lombardy [i.e. Italy]'.[14] Venice, rising obscurely in the course of the early Middle Ages from the waters to which she owed her immunity from attack, was nominally subject to the Byzantine Empire, in practice an independent city-state by the tenth century. Venice was unique in Christendom as a wholly commercial community: 'that people does not plough, sow nor gather grapes', as one surprised eleventh-century observer put it.[15] Venetian traders could negotiate favourable terms for trafficking with Constantinople; but they also dealt with the merchants of Islam. An early eleventh-century memorandum records that

When the Venetians come to Pavia [in Lombardy] they are required to render annually to the master of the treasury a pound each of pepper, cinnamon, galingale and ginger. And to the master's wife they must supply an ivory comb and a mirror and a set of dressing-table accessories.[16]

Characteristic products of the Islamic world, these are most likely to have been acquired by the Venetians in Egypt. What did they trade in return? We cannot be sure, but slaves, timber and salt were commodities perennially in demand in Cairo.

So between roughly 750 and 1000 there were plenty of interactions between Christendom and Islam. Some were violent and destructive; others were harmonious and fruitful. The crowded, jostling canvas contains warriors, diplomats, converts, merchants, pilgrims, scholars, artists, craftsmen and slaves. What is still strikingly absent is any sense that either side of the cultural divide was remotely interested in the religion of the other. Christians maintained a sullen hostility to the heretical Ishmaelites. Muslims found in Christendom a convenient source of scientific expertise or human commodity but were otherwise disdainful. (Possibly the intellectual circles of al-Ṭabarī in ninth-century Baghdad constitute some sort of rule-proving exception.) Christian and Muslim lived side by side in a state of mutual religious aversion. Given these circumstances, if religious passions were to be stirred up, confrontation would probably be violent.

3

Crossing Frontiers

In the course of the triumphant campaigns of the 'Byzantine reconquest' in the tenth century, when territories in Armenia, south-eastern Anatolia and northern Syria were successfully repossessed for the Empire, Byzantine soldiers were under orders to gather up copies of the Koran and burn them. By this period there had already existed for some time a 'mosque of the Saracens'[1] in the centre of Constantinople for the use of visiting diplomats, traders and prisoners-of-war. It is referred to in the handbook commissioned by Constantine Porphyrogenitus mentioned in the preceding chapter. What is more, the writer knew the correct term for it, in Greek *magisdion*, derived from Arabic *masjid*, our 'mosque'. There is a contrast here, perhaps not a surprising one, between the intolerant ethos of the camp and the more welcoming attitudes of the capital. In the study of Byzantine civilization it has always been a source of difficulty for historians that we know so much more about Constantinople than we do about the provinces. Have we any means of getting at the assumptions and attitudes that were held in those frontier marchlands where Christian and Muslim lived side by side?

The survival of a most remarkable poem, known after its hero as *Digenes Akrites*, enables us to return a cautious

Kiev•

R. Dnieper

R. Danube

•Brixen

•Venice

Nicopolis•

Black

Santiago de
Compostela•

Montpellier•   •Genoa
                  •Pisa

Constantinople•

CASTILE   •Barcelona   •Rome

SELJUK
TURKS

Toledo•

Smyrna•

Lisbon•   •Valencia   Amalfi•

Khios

•Córdoba   Palermo•

A L M O R A V I D S

•Granada

B A R B A R Y   C O A S T

•Mahdia

Tyre• 3

Tripoli•

4

•Marrakesh

F A T I M I D S

Cairo•

R. Nile

| o | 800km |
| o | 500miles |

——— Approximate boundaries of Byzantine Empire _c._1140

Ⓘ Crusading states of Outremer: 1 Edessa; 2 Antioch;
   3 Tripoli; 4 Jerusalem

——— Approximate frontier between Christian and Muslim
   in the Iberian Peninsula after the conquest of Lisbon (1147)

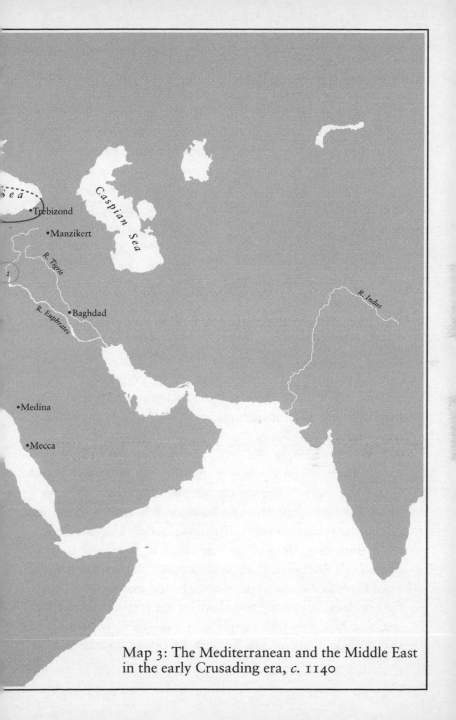

Map 3: The Mediterranean and the Middle East
in the early Crusading era, *c.* 1140

affirmative answer. The poem, variously styled an epic, a proto-romance or a series of ballads, celebrates the martial and amorous exploits of a hero named Basil, also known as *Digenes*, 'the twice-born', and *Akrites*, meaning 'a border soldier', 'a frontier guard' or 'a pacifier of the marches'. It is set in the distant eastern marchlands hundreds of miles from Constantinople. It is a poem as problematic as it is strange and haunting. In the written form in which it has come down to us it is most likely a composition of the period falling on either side of the year 1100. One may hope to find in it a mirror of some of the attitudes of that epoch. Basil owed his nickname 'twice-born' to the fact that, as the poet tells us, he was born 'of a gentile (i.e. Muslim) father and a Roman (i.e. Byzantine) mother'.[2] His father was in fact a Syrian emir who carried off Basil's mother in the course of a raid into the Empire. He was subsequently permitted by her family to marry her on condition that he became a Christian. Cross-cultural romance is an important theme in the poem: men and women change their religious allegiance for love and marriage. All sorts of cultural loyalties, indeed, seem to be rather fluid.

Take, for example, Book V, narrated by the twice-born hero himself. When a young man and, though already married, living in the marches on his own, he wants 'to travel into inner Syria'.[3] At an oasis he meets a beautiful, grieving girl. She tells him her story. The daughter of 'Haplorrabdes, the emir of everything',[4] she had fallen in love with one of her father's Roman captives and eloped with him. But he has abandoned her at the oasis, where she has now been waiting for ten days. A passing traveller, on his way to ransom his son who has been taken captive by the Arabs, has told her that five days previously he saw her lover attacked by a well-known brigand called Mousour, but rescued by the valiant young borderer (i.e. Digenes Akrites). At this moment their talk is interrupted by an attack from Arab marauders; our hero sees them off. To the girl's question he then confesses that he is indeed the borderer who slew Mousour and saved the life of her lover. He offers to escort her back to him so that they may get married, 'if the base Ethiops' faith you will deny'.[5] She explains that she has already become a Christian at the bidding of her lover, 'For nothing could I, by desire enslaved, / Not bring to pass of what was said by him.'[6] They set out together. In the course of their journey Basil seduces her: their lovemaking is against her inclinations, so we should perhaps think of the encounter as something close to rape. Afterwards, Basil feels ashamed of his conduct. He reunites the lovers and admonishes the man to be faithful(!). Then, conscience-stricken, he returns to his own wife, who suggests that they should move to another land. (Later, in Book VII, we are told about the splendid palace that Basil builds for himself beside the Euphrates, i.e. beyond the Empire's eastern frontier.)

The world of the poem was one in which people travelled, for diversion or on errands of mercy, across cultural frontiers. They changed their faith for love. The primary enemy is not the infidel but the marauder and the brigand. The Muslims, indeed, respect Basil: after his death (in Book VIII) his funeral is attended by nobles from Baghdad and Babylon. In only one passage in the entire work is Basil credited with waging *holy* war, when with God's help he 'put down all the Hagarenes' insolence';[7] but even there the context is not one of religious struggle but of the suppression of brigandage and the bringing of peace to troubled borderlands. The author evidently knew a certain amount about Islamic beliefs and customs, to which he alludes in a neutral, but not a hostile fashion.

An atmosphere comparable to that suggested in *Digenes Akrites* can be sensed on another frontier at the opposite end of the Mediterranean. The eleventh century was a time of upheaval in al-Andalus. The unitary Hispano-Muslim state governed from Córdoba, so imposing in its tenth-century prime, experienced disputed successions, civil war and fragmentation in the early eleventh century. Its place was taken by a number of petty principalities, typically based on cities such as Seville or Valencia and their surrounding countryside, known to historians as the *taifa* kingdoms. (The label is derived from an Arabic term meaning 'faction' or 'party'.) Endemic rivalry among the *taifa* statelets rendered them vulnerable. The rulers of the Christian kingdoms of northern Spain, especially the kings of León-Castile and the counts of Barcelona, quickly became skilful at exploiting these rivalries. By posing as the military protectors of the *taifa* rulers, they were able to extract prodigiously large sums in tribute. The flow of gold from Islamic into Christian Spain in the eleventh century was to have far-reaching consequences.

Kings were not the only people who profited from this protection racket. The most famous Spaniard of all time, Rodrigo Díaz, better known to history as El Cid, was an eleventh-century Castilian nobleman who had a spectacularly successful career as a freelance mercenary soldier. In his lifetime he was not what later legend would turn him into, a crusading patriot who strove to liberate his fatherland from the Moors. Far from it: a commander of genius, blessed by good fortune, he sold his skills to Muslim and Christian alike and ended up as the ruler of his own independent *taifa* principality based at Valencia. His career was reliably recorded not long after his death by an anonymous author, who showed no surprise that his hero should sometimes have been fighting in the pay of the Christian Alfonso VI of León-Castile, sometimes in that of the Muslim emir of Saragossa. The historical Rodrigo, like the legendary Basil, operated in marchlands where allegiances were negotiable.

We possess a strictly contemporary witness to the quality of the relations between Muslim and Christian in Spain at princely levels. This is nothing less than the autobiography of one of the rulers of the *taifa* states, 'Abd Allāh, emir of Granada from 1073 to 1090; a richly rewarding work, casting a flood of light upon the society and political life of al-Andalus in the eleventh century and revealing its author as all too human a being – relaxed, engaging, a good storyteller, frank about his weaknesses, a shade timorous. At several points, the author graphically describes the process of negotiating with Alfonso VI or his envoys. Here is his account of negotiations which took place in the winter of 1089–90:

Alvar Fáñez [one of the king's generals, and a relative of El Cid] had been entrusted by Alfonso with the regions of Granada and Almería, whether it was a question of attacking those [Muslim] princes who had failed to meet his demands, or of receiving money or of intervening in anything that might be of advantage to him. Alvar Fáñez at first sent a message to me on his own account threatening to enter Guadix and adding that only the payment of a ransom would deter him. I asked myself: 'Whose help can I get to protect me from this threat? How can I possibly keep him at bay when no troops have been left to help us defend ourselves?' [Several more panicky self-questionings follow.] I decided to placate Alvar Fáñez by making a small payment to him and at the same time concluded an agreement with him whereby he undertook not to come near any of my towns after he had received that payment. He undertook to abide by these terms but, on receiving the money, he observed: 'You're quite safe as far as I'm concerned. But it is more imperative that you placate Alfonso. Those who comply with his wishes will be safe, but he will set me on those who don't . . .'[8]

The atmosphere of demands and pleadings, of menace and threats, is nicely conveyed. By this stage of affairs, 'Abd Allāh was in an extremely jumpy state. And justifiably so: only a few months later he was to be deposed from his rule of Granada and packed off into exile. It was as exiled royalty that he composed his memoirs – something which needs to be borne in mind when reading them. But he was not deposed by King Alfonso, nor any other Christian authority. Rather, he met his downfall at the hands of a fellow Muslim, an invader from North Africa; and his memoirs were composed in Morocco.

This new actor on the scene was named Yūsuf, and he styled himself 'Emir of the Believers'. He was the leader of what today would be called a fundamentalist Islamic sect, known to us as the Almoravids – derived from an Arabic term meaning 'those who band together for the defence of the faith' – which had grown up in southern Morocco in the recent past. Ascetic, puritanical and intolerant, the Almoravids were shocked by the goings-on across the Straits in Spain where Muslims were being forced to pay tribute to non-Muslims and were raising taxes unsanctioned by the Koran in order to do so. Determined on purifying Islamic observance, Yūsuf crossed to Spain in 1086, inflicted a heavy defeat on King Alfonso, swept away the *taifa* rulers and installed the Almoravids in power. Thus was al-Andalus united once more, but this time under an authority more hostile to non-Muslims than any previous one.

At the same epoch the eastern Mediterranean lands were suffering comparable disruption. The new arrivals were the Seljuk Turks, a semi-nomadic people originating in Central Asia who migrated westwards in the eleventh century. The world they then entered had changed significantly since the glorious early days of the Abbasid caliphate where we left it back in the ninth century. Then, Islam had been united (excepting only the refugee emirate of Córdoba in the distant west): by the eleventh century it had fragmented. This was a long-range consequence of the rift within Islam between the Sunni and Shi'ite factions referred to in Chapter 1. The Shi'ite movement, growing obscurely in North Africa, had been able to lay hold of Egypt in the tenth century and found a rival caliphate at Cairo in 969. This new claimant to spiritual authority within the Islamic world was known as the Fatimid caliphate because the ruling dynasty claimed descent from the Prophet's daughter Fatima. Meanwhile in Baghdad, partly as cause, partly as consequence of the rise of the Fatimids, the Abbasid caliphate had been weakened by palace faction and military coups, the usual diseases of court-based political systems. Although the Abbasids continued to preside, they no longer governed. In these circumstances the fringes of the Abbasid polity, for example in Syria and Palestine, were left to their own devices and tended to fragment into effectively independent territorial emirates – not unlike the *taifa* states of al-Andalus – quarrelsome, vulnerable and of course coveted by their more powerful neighbours.

The Fatimid caliphate was one of those neighbours, and during the eleventh century it exercised a shifting and uncertain dominion in Palestine and Syria. The other neighbour was the Byzantine Empire. By the tenth century the Empire's ruling circles had patiently adapted to changed circumstances and clambered out of the trough of military reverse, economic stagnation and cultural strife which had characterized the previous three centuries. Now prosperous, confident and hawkish, the emperors embarked upon a programme of recovery. They were the leaders of the Chosen People of God, whose sacred duty it was to wage just and holy war for the repossession of rightfully Christian lands. Their generals took advantage of the frailties of Abbasid rule in northern Syria. In 969 – the same year as the foundation of the Fatimid caliphate in Egypt – Byzantine armies recovered Antioch, a city heavy with Christian associations. Under Basil II (976–1025) the Empire achieved the greatest territorial extent it had known since pre-Islamic days.

It was into this confused and unstable world that the Seljuk Turks made their way. It was of critical importance that when in the course of their migrations they adopted Islam, the branch of the faith that they chose was the Sunni. This meant that they saw themselves as loyal subjects of the Abbasid caliph in Baghdad. Their duty therefore was to reaffirm orthodox Sunni Islam in the face of its rivals. The principal rival was necessarily the heretical Fatimid caliphate in Egypt, and a long way after that came the Christian Byzantines and the medley of petty emirates, be they Arab, Kurdish, Bedouin, Armenian or whatever, in northern Iraq and Syria.

The Seljuks were formidable warriors, feared for their deadly skills as mounted archers. Their incursions into Byzantine Asia Minor from the middle years of the eleventh century onwards – not a systematic invasion but intermittent raids and gradual seepage – were seen in Constantinople as an affront which had to be punished. But the attempted reprisal went disastrously wrong. In 1071 a Byzantine army under the command of the Emperor Romanus was decisively defeated at Manzikert, near Lake Van in today's eastern Turkey. The Emperor himself was captured. The immediate consequences of the battle were unremarkable. The Seljuk sultan treated Romanus magnanimously and released him in return for a few border strongpoints and a heavy ransom. But in the longer term the consequences of the Battle of Manzikert were such as to justify ranking it as one of the most decisive encounters of history. It facilitated Turkish penetration of Asia Minor. This caused consternation among the governing circles of Constantinople, who launched appeals to western or Latin Christendom for military aid. The response took the form of what we call the Crusades, and among the consequences of the Crusades was the fatal weakening of the Byzantine Empire. The fall of Constantinople to Ottoman conquerors in 1453 stemmed from the Battle of Manzikert nearly four centuries earlier.

From time out of mind it had been Romano-Byzantine policy to hire foreign mercenary troops. These might be bands under their own leaders on short-term contracts, or permanent contingents directly under imperial control like the famous Varangian Guard recruited from Scandinavia and England. So when the Emperor Alexius I despatched envoys to Pope Urban II in 1095 seeking publicity for an appeal for military assistance, he was doing nothing new or out of the ordinary. We have a fairly good idea of the sort of response he was expecting: manageable bodies of well-armed and disciplined warriors who could be deployed under the command of his generals for specific military tasks. In the event what he got was an enormous rabble of zealous but for the most part uninstructed fighting men, unamenable to imperial control, who trampled across his territories and blundered on down into Syria and Palestine where they captured Jerusalem in July 1099. We call this the First Crusade. But the participants, of course, did not. They could have had no idea that they were taking part in an operation which would be the first of a series.

So what did they think they were doing? This is no occasion to be diverted into an investigation of crusading origins, fascinating though the quest is. All that it is necessary to state here is that when Pope Urban preached at the Church council of Clermont in November 1095 the sermon which precipitated military operations, his words struck chords which were already obscurely sounding in the hearts and minds of his audience. Precisely what those words were we cannot say, for there are conflicting contemporary reports of the Pope's address. But it is reasonably plain that he proclaimed that by undertaking an armed pilgrimage to Jerusalem the participants would not only bring succour to their Christian brethren in the east but would also acquire spiritual merit and earn themselves a place in paradise. Notions about pilgrimage, holy warfare, the threat to Christendom and the numinous sanctity of Jerusalem were not new: what the Pope did was to tie them all together in such a fashion as to make them irresistible to the unsophisticated piety of Western European knighthood.

The reaction to his words was conditioned in important ways by the fact that the most enthusiastic response came from the warrior aristocracy of northern Francia. These were people who knew little or nothing about Islam. We can attempt to eavesdrop on their attitudes by attending to the literature they appreciated, just as we tried to prise open the mentalities of the Byzantine marchlands with the aid of *Digenes Akrites*. The most rewarding work for this purpose is the Old French epic poem called the *Chanson de Roland* [Song of Roland] which survives in a manuscript of *c.* 1100 and which probably took on its final form not long before that date. The language of the poem is that of northern Francia, its theme is strife and combat among the Frankish elite, its tone is thoroughly aristocratic and its trappings are those of the eleventh century. By common consent it affords a glimpse into the assumptions of the warriors who partici-pated in the First Crusade. The poem took its cue, so to say, from a historical event, the defeat of the rearguard of Charlemagne's army, under the command of Roland, in the Pyrenean pass of Roncesvalles in the year 778 at the hands of local Basque tribesmen. But the poet or poets who sub-sequently reworked the story transformed it. The enemy became the Muslims of Spain; treachery became the turning point of the plot; Roland was elevated to heroic stature; and the militarily insignificant encounter at Roncesvalles all those years before was infused with the grandeur of a battle between Christendom and her foes. Those foes were identi-fied – incorrectly of course – as 'pagans', who worshipped idols called Mahoun, Apollyon and Tervagant (in a sort of parody of the Christian Trinity) in 'synagogues and mahum-eries'. The poet resoundingly stated that 'pagans are wrong and Christians are right'.[9] Pagans moreover are untrust-worthy, treacherous and cruel, natural enemies of the Christ-ian moral order. To fight them is to do meritorious penitential work. To die in battle with them is to win the crown of martyrdom. And such were the attitudes which underpinned the morale of the armies of the First Crusade.

The capture of Jerusalem in 1099 by such undisciplined troops was a fluke success which came about because the crusaders happened to invade Syria at a time of extreme disarray in that corner of the Islamic world. In its aftermath most of them drifted home. But something had to be done with the territories acquired. No one wanted to restore them to the Byzantine Empire: rifts between crusaders and Greeks had already opened in the course of the campaign, and this refusal to comply with the Emperor's expectations would widen them. Just enough crusaders stayed on in the east to set up independent Christian principalities there, collectively known as *Outremer* ('Across the Sea'). These were, running from north to south, the County of Edessa, the Principality of Antioch, the County of Tripoli and the Kingdom of Jerusalem. Vulnerable colonial offshoots, crippled from the start by shortage of manpower and of the economic resources requisite for effective government, the crusading states of Outremer immediately became the objects of Islamic counter-attack. Edessa was the first to go, recaptured for the *Dār al-Islām* in 1144 by Zengi, governor of Aleppo and Mosul in northern Syria (and in theory a deputy of the Seljuk sultan, in practice an independent Sunni ruler). The Second Crusade (1147–9) failed to repossess Edessa, did little to strengthen the states of Outremer, and gave rise to further bickerings between crusaders and Greeks.

With hindsight we can see that a decisive development occurred in the early 1170s. Zengi's son Nūr al-Dīn gained control of Egypt, with its inexhaustible agricultural wealth, in 1169. His Kurdish general Ṣalāḥ al-Dīn, better known in Christendom as Saladin, consolidated the Sunnite hold there over the next two years, finally doing away with the detested Fatimid caliphate in 1171. On Nūr al-Dīn's death in 1174

Saladin succeeded him as ruler of a combined principality of Syria and Egypt. The Islamic world of the eastern Mediterranean was once more united, and included, in Egypt, its richest province. For millennia before the commercial exploitation of oil changed all sorts of balances, it has been broadly true that he who holds Egypt controls the eastern Mediterranean.

This had two consequences for the crusading movement. First, Saladin and his successors were able to exert a pincer pressure upon the Christian states of Outremer. An early and resounding fruit of this was Saladin's victory at the Battle of Hattin and subsequent reconquest of Jerusalem in 1187. The Third Crusade (1190–92) did not succeed in taking it back, for all the spirited generalship of King Richard I 'the Lionheart' of England. Second, it became clear that the grand strategy of crusading would have to be reconsidered. Frontal assaults upon the inhospitable Syrian coastline were fraught with difficulty. The overland route through Asia Minor was long, arduous and dangerous and stirred up all sorts of tensions with the Byzantine Empire. The new strategic thinking focused instead on what came to be called the 'way of Egypt'. Establish a bridgehead in Egypt, it ran, to gain control of the enemy's resources, then march through northern Sinai to take Jerusalem from the south.

This new strategy made sound sense. However, it would require many ships to transport a viable crusading army with its horses, stores and victuals to Egypt; and this would be costly. This was what doomed the Fourth Crusade (1202–04). Venice agreed to provide the ships, but when the crusaders found that they could not pay the bill an impasse was reached. A way out of the difficulty seemed to be found when a Byzantine pretender offered generous financial terms to the crusaders in return for aid in seating him upon the imperial throne in Constantinople. This the crusading army duly did. But the whole deal unravelled in an almost unimaginably disastrous fashion. When the new emperor reneged on the deal the crusaders and the Venetians found themselves forced to help themselves. In 1204 the crusading army captured and plundered the city of Constantinople, packed the imperial government off into exile at Nicaea in Asia Minor and set up a rival, Latin, empire which lasted until 1261. It was a blow from which the Byzantine Empire never fully recovered, and which has soured relations between Greek and Latin Churches from that day to this.

The way of Egypt was tried again in the Fifth Crusade (1218–21) and yet again in the crusading expedition of King Louis IX of France (1248–50). But not even the massive resources and meticulous preparations of the French monarchy could deliver success. After this the game was nearly up for what was left of Outremer. Antioch fell to Islamic armies in 1268, Tripoli in 1289, and the last outpost of Acre in 1291. This was not the end of crusading – far from it – but it ended any permanent European military presence in the eastern Mediterranean for nearly six centuries.

Military confrontation between Christendom and the *Dār al-Islām* during the crusading era was not confined to the eastern Mediterranean. Already, before the First Crusade, warrior-adventurers from Normandy had established themselves in southern Italy. Gradually between 1060 and 1091 they wrested Sicily and Malta from Muslim hands. Some short-lived outposts on the Tunisian coast of North Africa would be added in the middle years of the twelfth century. In the Iberian Peninsula the territorial expansion of the Christian monarchies at the expense of their Muslim neighbours continued intermittently throughout the twelfth century. Steady progress was checked first by the Almoravids and then by a second wave of Moroccan zealots, confusingly similar in name, the Almohads, in the second half of the century. A decisive victory at Las Navas de Tolosa by Alfonso VIII of Castile in 1212 exposed southern Spain to Christian conquest. Córdoba fell into Castilian hands in 1236, Seville in 1248. Valencia was captured by King James I of Aragon in 1238. Meanwhile in Portugal, where Christian dominion had been carried to the line of the Tagus with the conquest of Lisbon in 1147, the Algarve was absorbed during the first half of the thirteenth century. By 1250 the only precariously independent Islamic state left in the Peninsula was the emirate of Granada.

The foregoing few paragraphs constitute an almost telegraphically brief outline of the military history of the crusading era. Elaborate and detailed histories of the Crusades have been written in the course of the last half-century or so by the distinguished schools of crusading historians which flourish in Britain, France, Germany and the United States. Such works are rendered possible by the extremely rich source materials, especially the contemporary narratives stimulated by the crusading expeditions. These narratives are remarkably varied. They include ambitious 'overview' treatments such as the *History of Deeds Done beyond the Sea* by Archbishop William of Tyre (d.1186) and its thirteenth-century continuations. There are the testimonies of participants in individual episodes such as the work known as the *Gesta Francorum* [Deeds of the Franks], the earliest of all crusading narratives, by an anonymous knight from southern Italy; or the account of the siege and conquest of Lisbon by an English priest who had taken part in that

Anglo-Portuguese venture. We have the autobiography of a crusading king, the *Llibre dels Feyts* [Book of Deeds] of James I of Aragon. We have the affectionate memoir of his master and friend Louis IX of France composed by Jean de Joinville, a work whose narrative of the fighting that followed the French landing in Egypt must rank as one of the most vivid descriptions of combat ever penned. And there is much, much more besides. There was enough to fill five substantial folio volumes in the standard nineteenth-century edition of crusading sources, and several new sources have been discovered since then. Medieval Christendom took an intense interest in the Crusades and regarded them as a subject for serious and sustained attention in their own right, a topic which had moral weight and dignity.

There is an interesting contrast here with medieval Islam. There is no Islamic historiography of the Crusades as such. For contemporary Islamic narrators the Crusades were not much more than skirmishes which inflicted pinpricks upon the fringes of the Islamic world. Crusaders came and went: their activities might be laconically noted by chroniclers, but not dwelt upon. The only personage in the Islamic world during the crusading epoch who was the focus of attention for historians and biographers was Saladin. This was because he was the prop of Sunni Islam, the restorer of the holy city of Jerusalem to Muslim hands, a leader of great personal qualities – and, it must be said, a master of favourable self-presentation; not *primarily* because of his military engagement with the crusading armies. A small indication of Islamic indifference is furnished by terminology. The crusaders were invariably labelled simply as *Franji*, 'Franks', whether they came from Sicily, Hungary or Scotland; no Arabic word was coined to indicate that these intruders were engaged in a special and individual form of warfare. The indifference of the medieval Islamic world to the Crusades is part and parcel of its indifference to the culture of Christendom at large.

Liberal critics of today are frequently to be heard denouncing the Crusades. A typical recent authority has described them as 'disgraceful'.[10] But rebuking the past from the different moral standpoint of the present does not advance historical understanding. During the crusading era no orthodox Christian writer ever criticized the Crusades as such. (A very few heretics did, usually on the grounds of pacifism.) There was plentiful criticism, but it was not about fundamental principles. It concerned the moral state and disposition of the crusaders, or the ways and means of organizing particular crusading campaigns. On the central issue that underlay crusading there was consensus: it was legitimate to seek to repossess the Holy Places for Christendom by military means, and it was meritorious for an individual actively to strive to that good end. Unpalatable as it may be to a modern understanding, this doctrine was accepted uncritically by millions of people of both sexes, from every walk in life and every rank of society, over several centuries.

Between 1050 and 1300 Christian dominion came and went in Syria and Palestine, returned to Sicily, and reabsorbed nearly all the Iberian Peninsula. The period had been one of permanent hostility – not quite the same thing as permanent war – between Christianity and Islam in the Mediterranean world. Does that mean that a wall of intolerance had been erected between Christian and Muslim? The answer to this question is not as straightforward as it might appear.

There was abundant religious enthusiasm in the course of the crusading epoch – the zeal of the recently-converted

Seljuk Turks, the fanaticism of the Moroccan sectaries, the bigotry of Frankish warriors and the rantings of Christian preachers. Religious zeal among the devotees of two monotheisms, each unshakeably convinced of its own righteousness, is by definition intolerant. Again, this was an epoch within western Christendom in the course of which the ecclesiastical hierarchy was defining norms of Christian observance more strictly, communicating them more widely, and devising means of enforcing them more effectively than ever before. It was thus becoming easier to identify deviants from orthodoxy, such as heretics, and to coerce them. There was more of a will to persecute in the Europe of 1300 than there had been in the Europe of 1000, and more refined techniques for doing so. Such attitudes necessarily rubbed off on to crusaders who were, after all, doing battle with what was still perceived as a Christian heresy (see Chapter 1). When the French troubadour Marcabrun sang in about 1150 of crusaders 'cleansing' lands of the enemies of Christ he was drawing on a new rhetoric which was to have a long life (and which we have come to distrust). Some fifty years later, when an unknown poet composed the Spanish epic *Poema de Mio Cid* he presented his hero in an entirely different light from that shone by the anonymous biographer referred to earlier in this chapter. All references to El Cid's mercenary exploits in Muslim service have been edited out. The past has been adjusted in the interests of the present. El Cid has become an exclusively Christian, crusading, Castilian patriot.

So far, so – apparently – straightforward. But there are complexities here. Hostility is itself a relationship, its rhythms and routines necessitating interactions. Take the Christian states of Outremer. Crippled from the outset by a shortage of manpower, their governing elites quickly realized that survival depended on diplomacy as much as it did on war. Diplomacy meant entering into guarded relations with Islamic neighbours; having dealings with the enemy. There were embassies to be exchanged, alliances to be negotiated, truces to be arranged, prisoners to be ransomed. Political and military intelligence had to be gathered and evaluated in the shadowy underworld of the spy. For obvious reasons such persons are rarely visible in our sources. Just occasionally, however, a curtain is drawn back. One of the contemporary chroniclers of the Third Crusade offers us a glimpse:

> Now while they were all promising
> What each man to the siege would bring
> And give, behold, Bernard, the spy,
> A man in Syria born, drew nigh;
> Of native-born he had two more
> With him. Saracen garb they wore.
> They were returned from Babylon [i.e. Cairo],
> Where they had, for sole mission,
> To spy upon the enemy;
> I say to you assuredly
> That more Saracen seeming folk
> I never saw, or men who spoke
> More perfectly Saracen speech.[11]

Bernard's fluency in Arabic, which fitted him for his dangerous job, was matter for remark. How widespread was bilingualism in Outremer? It is one of many important questions which the surviving sources do not permit us to answer. We can point to a few among its Christian inhabitants, such as Bernard, who are known to have had a knowledge of

Arabic. Another such person, at a much more exalted level, was Reynald of Châtillon, Prince of Antioch. As a prisoner-of-war he spent fifteen years in captivity in Aleppo, during which time he learned the language of his captors. Reynald was one among many of the elite of Outremer who adopted much of the manner of life of the Arab world. But it did nothing to make him more sympathetic to his Muslim neighbours after his release. A violent and unscrupulous man, Reynald was a violator of truces, an attacker of pilgrims making their way peacefully to Mecca. Captured again after the Battle of Hattin, he was executed for what we should today call his war-crimes by Saladin in person.

As a captive Reynald of Châtillon crossed frontiers involuntarily. Other exalted persons might cross them willingly. Consider the extraordinary trajectory of the Portuguese prince Dom Pedro (1187–1256). After unsuccessful intrigues to block the accession of his brother to the throne of Portugal in 1211, Pedro had to flee his native land. He took refuge at the court of his neighbour and kinsman by marriage, Alfonso IX of León. This was in the very year that preparations were being made for the campaign, proclaimed a Crusade by the pope, to be led by Alfonso's cousin, namesake and enemy the King of Castile, which would result in the great victory at Las Navas in the following year. Alfonso IX stood conspicuously aloof from that campaign, bribed, it was whispered, by Muslim gold sent by the Almohad ruler of Al-Andalus and Morocco. Whatever the truth or otherwise of this rumour, it is certain that at this period diplomatic relations between León and Morocco were warm. Perhaps unsurprisingly, therefore, Dom Pedro next turns up in Morocco. As a mercenary captain he commanded a foreign legion in the service of the Almohads between about 1216 and 1228. This did not put him beyond the pale. Returning to Spain he made his way to the court of King James of Aragon. He was able to assist the king in materially advantageous ways in the context of James's rather sordid matrimonial affairs. His reward, in 1231, was the lordship of Majorca, recently conquered from Islam. Pedro subsequently participated in the Aragonese conquests of Ibiza and Valencia. This remarkable career bears some resemblances to that of El Cid a century and a half beforehand. Yet it was played out in a cultural context which was finding El Cid's frontier-crossing exploits unacceptable and, as we have seen, adjusting his image accordingly.

Some crossed frontiers permanently. Jean de Joinville had an encounter in Egypt which shocked and saddened him. The meeting occurred during the negotiations which followed upon the defeat and capture of King Louis and the other crusading leaders at the Battle of Mansourah in the spring of 1250. Joinville describes how the King had been taken aback to be approached by a Saracen who had addressed him in fluent French:

When the King had asked him where he had learnt French the man replied that he had once been a Christian. Thereupon the King had said to him: 'Go away! I don't wish to speak with you any further!' I had drawn the man aside and asked him to tell me his circumstances. He had told me that he was born in Provins [about fifty miles south-east of Paris], and had come to Egypt; he had married an Egyptian and was now a person of great importance. 'Don't you realize,' I had said to him, 'that if you die in this condition you will be damned and go to hell?' He had replied that he knew it, and was moreover certain that no religion was so good as the Christian religion. 'But,' he had added, 'I'm afraid to face the poverty and shame I'd have to suffer if I returned to you. Every day someone or other would say to me: "Hullo, you rat!" So I prefer to live here rich and at ease than place myself in such a position as I can foresee.' I had pointed out to him that on the Day of Judgement, when his sin would be made plain to all, he would have to suffer greater shame than any he spoke of at that moment. I had given him much good Christian advice, but all to little effect. So he had left me, and I never saw him again.[12]

Prudent warriors have always respected the fighting qualities of their foes. The barons of the *Chanson de Roland* knew that their 'pagan' enemies were doughty fighters. The author of the *Gesta Francorum*, who had himself fought the Turks, conceded that 'you could not find stronger or braver or more skilful soldiers' than they.[13] Crusaders could respect moral as well as martial worth in their opponents. Saladin is the prime but not the only example, a man of his word, pious and wise, clement and just, terrible only to those, like Reynald of Châtillon, who flouted the laws of war. Joinville could quote Saladin's maxims with approval: 'Saladin said that you should never kill a man once you had shared your bread and salt with him.'[14] In the following century Dante located Saladin in Limbo among the virtuous non-Christians, in the distinguished company of Homer, Plato and Aristotle.

Traces of similar attitudes can be found on the Islamic side. It is once more Joinville who tells us of the reputation of King Richard the Lionheart:

King Richard became so noted for his daring exploits while overseas that when any horse belonging to a Saracen shied at a bush its master would say to it: 'D'you think that's King Richard of England?'[15]

Our most communicative witness to Islamic attitudes is another autobiographer, as revealing of his age as 'Abd Allāh of Granada was of his. Usāmah ibn Munqidh (1095–1188), emir of Shaizar in northern Syria, exceptionally long-lived, well-connected, widely-acquainted, has left us a vivid account of his experiences in his anecdotal memoirs. They furnish an especially valuable record of his encounters with the Franks of Outremer. Usāmah regarded the Franks as enemies, of course, but worthy ones. He routinely referred to them as 'The Franks – God confound them!'[16] He was contemptuous of some aspects of their culture, for instance their ignorance of medicine, and bewildered by others, for example the social freedom of Christian women. On the other hand, during periods of truce you could be friends with the Franks and find shared interests. Usāmah was a passionate sportsman and a keen observer of wildlife. This was a bond with the Frankish aristocracy: there are several casual references in his memoirs to hunting and hawking expeditions with Frankish friends. His father had entertained the Frankish king of Jerusalem at Shaizar, and Usāmah himself was a regular visitor to the royal court, sometimes as a diplomat but on at least one occasion, intriguingly, as a litigant in a civil action against a Frankish baron concerning grazing. A courtroom dispute about herds of cattle sets Christian–Muslim relations in the crusading states in an unexpected light: it is right to keep our expectations open. Usāmah's work stands alone, and presents therefore the usual problems about how far we may generalize from it. It is prudent to be cautious. Yet when all is said and done it is hard to believe that Usāmah's attitudes were wholly unique.

*

It is usual to present the age of the Crusades as a time of mounting antagonism between Christian and Muslim. The pre-crusading era of the historical 'Abd Allāh and Rodrigo Díaz and of the fictional Digenes Akrites was characterized by a spirit of live-and-let-live. Zeal was infused with the irruption of invaders from outside the Mediterranean world, whether from Central Asia, northern Christendom or West Africa, unleashing explosive passions of hostility. The moral tone of the ensuing crusading era was epitomized by the thuggery of Reynald of Châtillon or the icy fanaticism of Louis IX. That is one way of interpreting the epoch. However, the example of men like Usāmah ibn Munqidh or Dom Pedro of Portugal suggests that matters might not be quite so clear cut. We might do well to bear in mind that human moral relationships usually have rather fuzzy outlines.

A less woeful way of looking at the Crusades lies in an appreciation of their role in opening up awareness of a larger world. When the armies of the First Crusade entered Syria and Palestine they encountered religious communities of an exotic kind which were strange to them. These might be Christians of the Churches of the East, such as the Monophysites (or Copts) and others. They might indeed be adherents of an entirely different confessional tradition, such as the Samaritans. Western and eastern Christians were not of much interest to one another. If anything, the establishment of Crusading principalities in Outremer threatened to disrupt the reasonably harmonious relations between the Christians of the East and their Islamic political masters: so the would-be succourers of the eastern Christians were eyed at best rather warily by those they came to help. Westerners regarded eastern Christians with hauteur, as remote and unappealing kinsfolk whose peculiar customs and traditions it was best to keep at arm's length.

Attitudes were more accommodating, however, towards even more distant and exotic Christian communities. In 1145 a visiting bishop from Outremer told the pope that he had heard tell of an eastern potentate of fabulous wealth and power, a Christian, allegedly descended from one of the Magi who had visited the infant Jesus at Bethlehem. This mysterious ruler, whose name was John, was eager to come to the aid of the Christians of Outremer by attacking their Islamic enemies from the east. This is the first appearance in historical record of the legend of Prester (i.e. *Presbyter*, or 'Priest') John. Twenty years later a letter allegedly from Prester John himself was brought to Europe. In it he described himself as the ruler of 'the Three Indias' and announced his intention of bringing military aid to defeat the enemies of Christendom. This hoax – for such it was – deceived many from the pope downwards, precisely because it was just what Christian leaders wanted to believe: a mighty Christian ally far to the east whose armies could take Islam in the rear and thereby facilitate repossession of the Holy Places by crusaders from the west. The legend of Prester John would persist for centuries, his elusive kingdom being variously located in Asia, India or Africa, a will-o'-the-wisp to be vainly pursued by fantasists who sought the deliverance of Christendom from its Muslim enemies.

The initial reports about Prester John, however, may have had their basis in real events. In 1141 the ruler of the Central Asian Qara-Khitai Empire – from which our term 'Cathay' derives – had defeated the Seljuk ruler of Persia. As rumours of these events filtered through to the beleaguered Christians of Outremer it must have been irresistible to cast the victor as a Christian ruler of a sort and thus a potential ally against Islam. In 1177 Pope Alexander III despatched an embassy to Prester John. It can be traced through Outremer, but thereafter was never heard of again. Had diplomatic links been forged on this occasion between Christendom and – well, somewhere in the distant east – the shock of what next came out of Central Asia might have been lessened.

What came next was the assault of the Mongols. The Mongol Empire was like nothing in the world's history before or since. Under a leader named Tumüchin the Mongol tribes were united during the years on either side of 1200, after which Tumüchin assumed the title of Chingiz or Genghis Khān, which means 'universal ruler'. The unification of the Mongol tribes resulted in the creation of a first-rate army. This military machine had to be put to use. The maintenance of unity required external conquests. This is the most convincing explanation of Mongol expansion. Before his death in 1227 Genghis subjugated northern China to his east, and to the west the Qara-Khitai and the Islamic polities of northern Iran. Expansion continued after his death. Under his son Ögedei (1229–41) the Mongol conquests in northern China were consolidated. In the late 1230s another western offensive was launched. The southern Russian principalities were overrun, Kiev being sacked in 1240, and the Mongol advance continued unstoppably into Hungary, Poland and even Germany. It was only Khān Ögedei's death in 1241 that caused his commanders to abandon the assault on Western Europe.

By the 1240s the Mongol Empire extended from eastern Europe to the Pacific. If it was manifestly not the empire of Prester John, it invited investigation from frightened Europeans, if only in the interests of self-defence. The matter was discussed at the highest level at the Ecumenical Council of Lyons presided over by Pope Innocent IV in 1245. As a result of these deliberations three embassies were despatched to the Mongols. Their briefs were to open diplomatic relations, to observe and report on the Mongols, and to make contact with eastern Christian communities. Larger and mistier hopes focused upon the linked possibilities that the Mongols might be persuaded to abandon the shamanism which seems to have been their religion and to adopt Christianity. They would then be able to undertake military action in concert with the West against Middle Eastern Islam. The Mongols matter in the history of Christian–Islamic relations in the Middle Ages because it was seriously believed in the highest circles in the thirteenth century that they might be turned into Prester John.

In the event these fervently entertained hopes proved completely illusory. Although a number of influential Mongols did adopt Nestorian Christianity, there was never any likelihood of the Mongols as a whole embracing the Catholic Christianity of Europe.* Indeed, the Mongols soon turned away from the West. The much-feared Mongol assault never took place, perhaps for what would today be called ecological or environmental reasons: the millions of Mongol horses depended on the pasture provided by steppe lands such as do not exist in sufficient abundance west of the Ukraine. The Mongol invasion of Iraq did lead to the capture and sack of Baghdad and the deposition and murder of the last Abbasid

---

* The Nestorians were another among the Churches of the east. Nestorius, Patriarch of Constantinople (428–31), was deposed for allegedly heretical opinions. His followers sought asylum in the lands to the east of the Roman Empire and formed a strong base in Mesopotamia. From there Nestorian communities spread across Central Asia to China.

caliph in 1258. But this was in no sense a 'crusading' campaign concerted with the West. Two years afterwards a Mongol army was defeated at 'Ayn Jālūt in Galilee by the Mamlūks of Egypt (the Islamic dynasty that had succeeded Saladin's). But their subsequent withdrawal from Syria was a foregone conclusion: lack of extensive pasture made the Mediterranean borderlands as unappealing as agrarian Europe. The unitary Mongol Empire created by Genghis had already started to fray. In the second half of the thirteenth century it fell apart into separate polities in China, Central Asia, Persia and Russia.

However, the contacts initiated in the 1240s had been made, the reports drafted. These reports are of the greatest interest. The most remarkable among them is that composed by the Franciscan missionary William of Rubruck, despatched by Louis IX of France, who visited the Mongol Khan Möngke – grandson of Genghis – in the years 1253–5. Rubruck's account is one of the world's great pieces of travel writing. Shrewd and observant, he set down for his royal master a detailed account of his travels, always difficult and often dangerous, across thousands of miles of – for a European – utterly unfamiliar territory, and of the strange and exotic people he encountered, their appearance, customs and beliefs. Rubruck's meticulous description of the unfamiliar seems to look forward to much later ethnographic and anthropological writing. Here he is describing the dwellings of the Mongols:

The dwelling in which they sleep is based on a hoop of interlaced branches, converging at the top around a smaller hoop, from which projects a neck like a chimney. They cover it with white felt: quite often they also smear the felt with chalk or white clay and ground bones to make it gleam whiter, or sometimes they blacken it. And they decorate the felt around the neck at the top with various fine designs . . . These dwellings are constructed of such a size as to be on occasions thirty feet across: I myself once measured a breadth of twenty feet between the wheel-tracks of a wagon, and when the dwelling was on the wagon it protruded beyond the wheels by at least five feet on either side. I have counted twenty-two oxen to one wagon, hauling along a dwelling, eleven in a row, corresponding to the width of the wagon, and another eleven in front of them. The wagon's axle was as large as a ship's mast, and one man stood at the entrance to the dwelling on top of the wagon, driving the oxen.[17]

Some of their draught animals were unfamiliar:

They have extremely strong cattle, with tails which are abundantly hairy like a horse's and with shaggy bellies and backs: they are shorter in the leg than other cattle, but stronger by far. They haul along the large dwellings of the Mongols, and have long slender twisted horns which are extremely sharp so that the points constantly require to be sawn off.[18]

It is the earliest European description of the yak.

William of Rubruck was not alone in looking with wonder upon the strangeness of the world to which God had called him and describing it accurately for his primary readership at the French royal court. (The surviving manuscripts suggest that Rubruck's work circulated in England too.) Joinville's *Life of St Louis* was completed in 1309 when the author was a very old man, but the major part of it was probably composed some forty years earlier. Joinville's description of places and peoples encountered while on crusade with his king in Egypt and Syria has an extraordinary freshness, a spring in its step that bounds across the seven centuries that separate him from us, vividly conveying the sense of a writer who looked keenly upon his world with an intense interest in all it had to offer him. Here he is describing a fossil fish:

During the king's stay at Saida someone brought him a stone that split into flakes. It was the most marvellous stone in the world, for when you lifted one of the flakes you found the form of a sea-fish between the two pieces of stone. This fish was entirely of stone, but there was nothing lacking in its shape, eyes, bones, or colour to make it seem otherwise than if it had been alive. The king gave me one of these stones. I found a tench inside; it was brown in colour, and in every detail exactly as you would expect a tench to be.[19]

Finally there is Marco Polo, the most famous of all European travellers of the Middle Ages. Marco belonged to a family of travellers. His father Niccolò and uncle Maffeo had undertaken a business trip from Constantinople to the Crimea in 1260 which unexpectedly took them on to Central Asia and China, from which they returned in 1269. Accompanied this time by the young Marco, they set out again in 1271, on this occasion as the accredited representatives of the pope, bearing diplomatic messages for the Khan Qubilai of China (Coleridge's Kubla Khan). Some three and a half years later the party reached Qubilai's summer residence of Shang-tu (Xanadu). The Polos remained in China for the next seventeen years. During this time Marco seems to have held some sort of post in the imperial bureaucracy, perhaps as a fiscal official, and was able to travel and observe frequently. In about 1291 the Polos were commissioned to escort a princess to Iran, and did so by way of the South China Seas, Java, Sumatra, Ceylon, India and the Straits of Hormuz. After this they returned home via Tabriz, Trebizond and Constantinople, finally reaching Venice in 1295. Marco then had his travels written up for him (and somewhat embellished) by a ghost-writer, Rustichello of Pisa.

Awareness of the bigness and strangeness of the world as evidenced in the writings of Rubruck, Joinville and Marco Polo (and several more besides from the period c.1250–1320) was an important development in the growth of the European mind. The mental horizons of the eleventh-century warriors who listened to the *Chanson de Roland* were narrow and ignorant. But by the early fourteenth century quite considerable numbers of westerners were aware that the world also contained mountains and seas, animals and peoples, customs and beliefs, that were almost unimaginably different from what was familiar at home. It cannot be wholly coincidental that the same period should have left us evidence of the first faint dawnings of the notion that there might be a plurality of religions in the world as well. This was a critically important development in the maturing of the mind of European Christendom. But before we can approach it there is some catching up to do in other areas of enquiry. What were Venetian businessmen like the Polos doing traversing the Old World eastwards to Peking and Xanadu? When we last glimpsed Venetian merchants, about the year 1000, they were only just beginning to nose their way down the Adriatic towards Constantinople and Alexandria. Much had happened since then.

4

Commerce, Coexistence
and Scholarship

Sometime in about the 1050s a Jewish lady in Jerusalem wrote to her supplier in Egypt to place an order for 'Shadhūna qirmiz'. Shadhūna is Medina Sidonia in southern Spain. Qirmiz is a dyestuff produced by crushing the beetle *Coccum ilicis* which lives in the bark of ilex trees; our word 'crimson' is derived from it. About three-quarters of a century later, to be precise on 11 August 1125, an Alexandrian merchant named Ibn Halīf died at Almería in south-eastern Spain in the course of a business trip. We know of these events owing to a chance documentary survival and an inscribed tombstone. They offer two minor examples of the commercial unity of the Mediterranean in that age, with goods and people flowing from one end of it to the other, and of the hegemony within it of Islamic and Jewish businessmen.

It was a hegemony that was already being challenged by rivals from the Christian world; specifically and initially from Italy. As we saw in Chapter 2, merchants from Amalfi and Venice were already in the tenth century venturing to the harbours of Egypt in search of the luxuries which the moneyed classes of Western Europe wanted. Others soon followed suit. Pisa's trade with Tunisia was so well established by the 1060s that a Jewish trader writing to a colleague could refer casually to a sale of pepper in al-Mahdīyya (Mahdia, on the coast between Sfax and Sousse in modern Tunisia) for Pisan currency. This was a turbulent commercial scene, in which the stakes were high and the risks great. Trade and piracy went hand in hand. In 1087 the Pisans, joined for the occasion by contingents from Genoa and Amalfi, attacked and plundered al-Mahdīyya and sailed home with much booty, some of which went to embellish their Campo Santo. Some historians have seen in this raid a sort of proto-Crusade.

So it is no wonder that Italian merchants were quick to seize the opportunities offered by the First Crusade and the establishment of the principalities of Outremer. These fledgling outposts were vulnerable. They needed ships to supply them with basic necessities such as food and weaponry. Only the Italians could do this. The Genoese were quickest off the mark: a full year before the conquest of Jerusalem they had extracted from the new Norman prince of Antioch a warehouse in that city, together with thirty dwellings, a well and a church, free of all rents and taxes – so highly was their maritime support valued.

The Venetians had concentrated their efforts upon breaking into the commercial zone of the Byzantine Empire in the Aegean and the Black Sea. Already before the end of the tenth century they had negotiated a trade treaty. But their really significant breakthrough occurred nearly a century later, when they were able to take advantage of the fact that the authorities in Constantinople had short-sightedly allowed the navy to run down. As the Seljuk Turks quietly gobbled up the hinterland of Anatolia in the wake of the Battle of Manzikert in 1071, the emperors needed to reinforce the coastal cities of Asia Minor. Simultaneously,

Brixen

R. Danube

Venice

Montpellier • Genoa

Nicopolis

BLACK

Kosovo

Barcelona

OTTOMANS • Constantino

Segovia

Gallipoli

Granada

Khíos • Smyrna

Ceuta

MERINIDS

Tripoli

Acre

Alexandria •

MAMLŪ

R. Nile

0   800 km
0   500 miles

Approximate frontier between Christian and Muslim in the Iberian Peninsula

Remaining fragments of the Byzantine Empire

Ottoman dominions

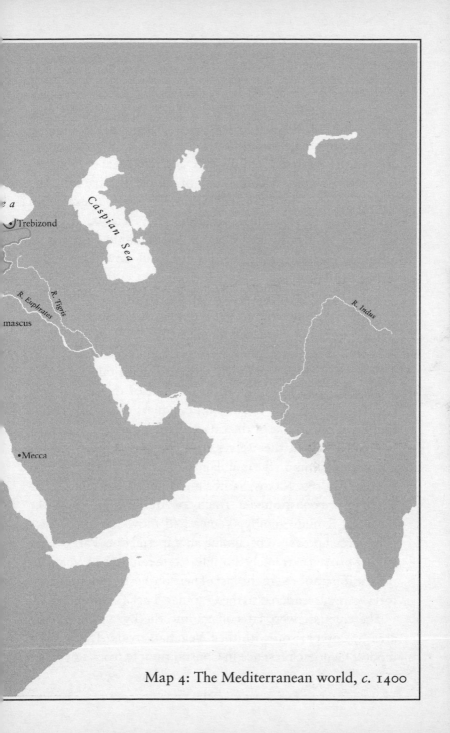

e a

Trebizond

Caspian Sea

R. Euphrates

R. Tigris

R. Indus

mascus

•Mecca

Map 4: The Mediterranean world, *c.* 1400

the Empire was threatened by new foes from the west. The Normans had established themselves on former Byzantine territory in southern Italy and Sicily, thereby engendering a state of mutual hostility between themselves and the imperial government in Constantinople. In 1081 a Norman army crossed the Adriatic, seized Corfu and laid siege to Durazzo (Durrës, on the Adriatic coast of modern Albania). The Venetians came to the rescue of the Empire, but exacted a heavy price. The trading privileges they secured in 1082 put them in a position of nearly unassailable commercial advantage which, with various ups and downs, lasted a century and more.

They did not neglect, during the twelfth century, the opportunities opening up in Outremer. Privileged Venetian trading quarters were negotiated at the maritime cities of Acre and Tyre – and they were very privileged indeed. At Tyre the Venetians demanded, secured and jealously guarded a full third part not only of the city but of its surrounding countryside too. After the Latin conquest of the Byzantine Empire in the course of the catastrophic Fourth Crusade the Venetians helped themselves to numerous Aegean islands and strongpoints on the mainland of the Peloponnese – Crete, Evvoia, Andros, Naxos, Santorini, Methóni, Koróni . . . The islands were constituted a 'Duchy of Archipelago' under the powerful Sanudo family. Venice had moved from being a commercial power to becoming an imperial one. Parts of her empire proved extremely durable. Crete remained a Venetian possession until 1669; the last of her southern Peloponnesian forts were surrendered to the Ottoman Turks as late as 1718.

The Genoese were latecomers into the Byzantine trading area by comparison with their Venetian rivals. There was a modest Genoese presence in Constantinople from 1155, but their big chance did not come until a century later. In 1261 they assisted in the restoration of a Greek emperor to Constantinople and were rewarded with trading privileges at the expense of the Venetians. Thereafter there was intense rivalry between the two for commercial pre-eminence. Genoese bases were to be found not only at Constantinople but also in the Aegean, the Crimea and on the coast of the Black Sea at Trebizond. Some of these, too, were to prove long-lasting. The Genoese held the island of Khíos, for example, until 1566. Genoese merchants were active also nearer home, in the central and western Mediterranean. In the middle years of the twelfth century Genoese investment in trading ventures to Sicily was exceeded only by those to Egypt and Outremer; and already there was modest but still significant investment in Spain, Tunisia, Algeria and Morocco. (We can reconstruct these investment patterns in some detail because of the fortunate survival of registers kept by commercial notaries from the second half of the twelfth century.) Genoese merchants even began to venture outside the Straits of Gibraltar and feel their way down the Atlantic coastline of Morocco. Soon some among them would be even more daring. In 1291 the Vivaldi brothers set out 'for the regions of India by way of the Ocean'.[1] They were never heard of again. Two centuries later another Genoese merchant explorer would be more successful.

Historians have traditionally tended to write about medieval commerce in the Mediterranean world as if it were almost exclusively the concern of the merchants of Italy. This concentration on Venetians, Pisans and Genoese has had the effect of sidelining others. There were enterprising merchants in several southern French cities, foremost among them Marseilles, and in the towns of eastern Spain, above all Barcelona.

A surviving register of contracts from 1248 shows that a single ship from Marseilles carried a consignment of (mainly) textiles to Outremer, many of them of local manufacture (Avignon, Narbonne, Tarascon), but some of them from much further afield, including bales of the famous cloth from Stamford in England. Barcelona was one of the great urban success stories of the twelfth and thirteenth centuries. Coastal trading up and down the Mediterranean littoral expanded into further-flung networks, trade and the flag being inextricably tied together as the rulers of the federation known as the *Corona de Aragón*, the 'Crown of Aragon', built up a maritime empire embracing the Balearic Islands (1229–32), Sicily (1282) and parts of Sardinia. Catalan mercantile stations were also to be found strung along the coast of North Africa. By 1300 the reach of Barcelona's canny business community stretched south across the Sahara and as far east as the Black and Red Seas.

Some of these colonial outposts were in themselves a source of commodities of trade. Outremer itself was not particularly productive, though the silk produced at Antioch, Tripoli and Tyre made its way to the West, as did the sugar – then a great luxury – grown in the Jordan Valley. The Genoese imported alum – vital as a fixing agent in the dyeing of cloth – from Smyrna and Trebizond to the weavers and fullers of western Christendom. Their island of Khíos was the principal source of mastic, an aromatic resin much in demand as part toothpaste, part chewing gum, among Europe's rich and chic.

However, the most significant feature of this surge of commercial activity, and in many respects the motor which drove it, was the gaining of access to trade routes whose furthest extremities lay in exotic countries where no European merchant had yet set foot. The northern parts of crusading Outremer lay at the western end of an overland route that stretched all the way across northern Mesopotamia and Iran to Central Asia and eventually China, the road that would be trodden by the Polos in the thirteenth century. Merchants based in Egypt could sail down the Red Sea and into the Indian Ocean. The Florentine Francesco Pegolotti, who edited a handbook for merchants in about 1330, listed nearly 300 'spices', the majority of which would have been imported into Mediterranean Europe from further east. 'Spice' was an elastic term which included pharmaceutical ingredients, cosmetic materials, dyestuffs and exotic fruits, as well as culinary spices proper. Pegolotti's list is a revelation of what the West wanted in his day (and was prepared to pay high prices for): cinnamon, cumin, dates, fenugreek, ginger (five types), indigo, madder, musk, opium, sandalwood, silkworm eggs, turpentine . . . Meanwhile, at the other end of the Mediterranean, in the cities of the Barbary Coast, the Genoese and Catalans could swing on the northern end of ropes of commerce which stretched across the Sahara to the gold, the ivory and the slaves which were to be had in markets like Timbuktu on the Niger.

In this manner, between about 1050 and 1250, a Western European and Christian mercantile hegemony gradually supplanted the Muslim–Jewish–Greek one which had previously held sway. Though subsequently threatened in more than one epoch, for instance by the expansion of the Ottoman Turks (see Chapter 5), this supremacy was never to be overthrown. It had far-reaching consequences. The linking of Mediterranean commerce with the maritime trade of northern Europe, combined with the advance of financial techniques and infrastructures (commercial partnerships, credit facilities, banking, accounting, marine insurance, etc.), brought into being the European mercantile capitalism which would later on achieve world dominance.

These developments are no part of our story. What *is*, however, is the baffling question of causation. How was it that Western merchants were able to overtake their rivals in those central medieval centuries? There is no obvious answer. The political resurgence of Christendom in the Mediterranean – Crusades, Sicily, Spain – did not deliver that sea, as some historians have claimed it did, to Western 'control'. Untamed piracy remained endemic there until the nineteenth century. The notion of 'control' of the Mediterranean before the modern age (or even, perhaps, within it) does not make much sense. In most of the resources that underpin commerce – technology, skills, commodities, attitudes – the Islamic world was vastly better endowed than Christendom, though the West was fast catching up (as we shall see shortly). The argument that commerce flourishes most readily in societies which have developed institutions capable of delivering peace, order and stability looks superficially more promising. On a large and general view medieval Christendom slowly attained this state, while the Islamic Mediterranean – but not other parts of the Islamic world – slowly lost it. But the argument breaks down on closer scrutiny. The most institutionally advanced states of medieval Europe were not to be found in the Mediterranean zone of the commercial revolution, but further to the north. Italy and the Crown of Aragon were not notable for peace, order and stability during the medieval period. A variant on this argument deserves pondering. Cities governed by merchants for merchants, whether as independent republics (Venice) or as communities largely running their own affairs under wisely non-interventionist monarchs (Barcelona), will strive to encourage commerce. Cities such as this flourished in Mediterranean Christendom. Why did they not flourish in the Islamic Mediterranean? That remains an open question, and one which opens up distant perspectives.

Businessmen from different cultures have to talk to each other. We don't know how they did so, in the literal sense of the language they used. The number of 'commercial Arabic' terms which passed into modern European languages suggests an international dialect of the mercantile community. For example, several of the terms for 'customs' in the Romance languages – *aduana*, *dogana*, *douane* and so forth – derive from the Arabic (originally Persian) *dīwān* meaning 'an account book' and so by extension a government department containing such things; a registry. Another pointer to the shared culture of the mercantile world lies in the diffusion of 'Arabic' numerals – they were originally Indian – in the course of the thirteenth and fourteenth centuries.

We do not know, because we have not got the sort of sources that would tell us, what the mood of these encounters might have been. Did Islamic and Christian merchants meet one another with suspicion? With strained joviality? With the guarded friendship that a landed aristocrat like Usāmah ibn Munqidh enjoyed with his sporting acquaintance among the Franks of Outremer? We ask such questions in vain.

About the tone of other sorts of relationship we know more. About rulers and ruled, for example. The political expansion of Christendom in the Mediterranean during the crusading epoch posed an unfamiliar question for governing circles in both state and Church. How do you set about administering communities of people of an alien culture? A contrast is often drawn between Islamic and Christian precept in this respect. As we have seen in Chapter 1, Islamic law decrees toleration for 'People of the Book'. Christian law does no such thing, with the result that treatment of conquered Muslim peoples depended on the whim of authority. In practice the contrast was not quite so clear cut as divergent precepts might suggest. People of the Book experienced various forms of restriction under Islamic rule, in the aggregate fairly vexatious. They were emphatically second-class citizens. Furthermore, the lowering of their status was progressive as time went by. The linked processes of conversion to Islam and of the emergence of a more open Islamic society (see Chapter 2) had the effect of closing off some of the spheres of influence previously colonized by People of the Book. The bureaucratic careers of John of Damascus and his forebears in the seventh and eighth centuries would have been well-nigh inconceivable in the eleventh or twelfth (though not under the Mongols in the thirteenth, but that is a different story).

On the other side of the cultural divide, the potential for harshness in the unfettered exercise of caprice or whim was tempered – not invariably, of course, but frequently – by the pressures of circumstance. The most significant such pressure was the need to retain a subject population in place as a labour force. The native Muslims of rural Outremer were in general not displaced but encouraged to stay and work the land. The Christian elite chose, for safety, to live in fortified towns and castles. In the countryside farming life went on much as it had always done: rents and dues were paid as before, but to new masters. This does not mean that all was harmony. Muslims under Christian rule, like Christians under Muslim rule, were subject to various discriminatory measures, for example as regards the type or colour of clothing they might or might not wear. Converts from Islam to Christianity might cross the social barriers erected (though not necessarily with ease, nor invariably finding a welcome). Subjects who maintained their Islamic loyalties were mistrusted and kept at a distance.

In the central and western Mediterranean lay regions where the coexistence of Muslim with Christian lasted longer than it had in the short-lived crusader principalities of Outremer. When Norman adventurers conquered Sicily in the eleventh century they found themselves the masters of a mixed population of Muslims and Christians (the latter for the most part Greek rather than Latin in religious observance). Courtly patronage encouraged an intermingling of cultures which yielded notable achievements in scholarship and beautiful ones in the arts, the latter exemplified by, for example, the cathedral of Monreale, near Palermo, built between 1174 and 1189. We must not leap to the conclusion that this was a harmonious society. Many Muslims who could afford to do so emigrated to Africa in the course of the twelfth and thirteenth centuries (just as at an earlier date many Christians had migrated from Africa to Christian Italy – see Chapter 2). The lowly Muslims who remained chafed under Christian rule. In the wake of a prolonged revolt the Emperor Frederick II – at this juncture the kingdom of Sicily was yoked uneasily to the Holy Roman Empire of Germany – in 1223 deported most of the remaining Muslim population of the island, some 20,000 people, to the south Italian mainland where they were little by little assimilated into Christian culture. It was a solution which in some respects foreshadowed the expulsion of the Moriscoes from Spain nearly four centuries later.

Islamic teaching encouraged emigration. 'The obligation

to emigrate from the lands of unbelief will continue right up to the Day of Judgement.'[2] So ran a legal ruling attributed to the jurist and scholar Ibn Rushd of Córdoba, better known in the West as Averroës. Some emigrated voluntarily. The Muslim exodus from Saragossa after its conquest by the Aragonese in 1118 left it a ghost town. Others left under compulsion. The Castilian conquerors of Seville in 1248 expelled every Muslim from the city in an act of what would later be called ethnic cleansing designed to render it exclusively Christian. But the sequel is striking. The policy practised at Seville was soon reversed. The conquerors could not make the city function without allowing its inhabitants to return and assist in peopling it. As in Outremer so in Spain, Christian authorities wanted defeated Muslims to stay on and work. Those who stayed on were known by the Arabic term *al-mudajjar*, meaning 'permitted to remain', which has yielded the Spanish word *mudéjar*, used by modern historians (both as noun and adjective) to characterize the culture of Muslims who lived under Christian rule in the Iberian Peninsula.

The geographical distribution of the Mudejars was far from even. For example, there were hardly any in Catalonia, while in neighbouring Valencia – the region rather than the city – the Mudejars vastly outnumbered the Christians, perhaps by as much as five to one, and an Islamic identity in faith, language and culture would persist for centuries. Valencia was in this respect untypical. In other parts of Spain and Portugal an Islamic identity was a good deal harder to maintain. Emigration of the Islamic elite, as from Sicily, removed not every single one but very many among the Muslim community leaders. Confiscation of the principal mosque of a conquered city, and frequently its conversion into a Christian cathedral as at Córdoba, loosened the social cohesion maintained by regular community worship. Mudejars were generally persons of lowly economic and social status, typically following callings such as muleteer, bricklayer, laundrywoman, gardener, potter. They enriched the Romance vernaculars with thousands of words derived from Arabic, and enriched peninsular craftsmanship with work in plaster and wood, tile and ceramic, but were not allowed to join the ruling culture except by paying the price of conversion. Like People of the Book under an Islamic dispensation, Muslims under Christian rule were second-class citizens, discriminated against in ways which made their subjection plain and were perhaps designed to humiliate. Mudejars could play no part in the municipal administration of the towns in which they dwelt. They were discriminated against at law in various ways, for example in that lower monetary penalties were exacted for crimes against them, so that, to put it crudely, it was cheaper for a Christian to steal from a Muslim than from a fellow Christian. They could easily fall into slavery – the entire population of Minorca was enslaved upon its conquest in 1287 – and legal obstacles were devised to hinder their attaining freedom. When the Host was carried through the streets in public processions they were required to fall to their knees. Artists liked to portray them in submissive postures. King Sancho IV of Castile (1284–95) observed in the book of advice composed for his son that 'the Moor is simply a dog and the Mooress a bitch'.[3]

Attentive scrutiny of the above examples will show that several among them are what we call 'normative' or 'prescriptive', that is to say they are drawn from legal enactments, and these may not be reliable guides to everyday social reality. Or they may. How is the historian to tell? To give a simple example, when Spanish municipal regulations required apartheid at the town baths, different days for Christians, Muslims and Jews, are we to assume that the ruling was thought to be necessary because it was not being observed? Or might it have been enacted for some completely different reason, for instance a fiscal one, so that the authorities could fine a bath-house keeper accused of infringing it?

The example of the municipal baths reminds us that what historians call by the Spanish term *convivencia*, the 'living side by side' of Christian and Muslim in medieval Spain and Portugal, reached down to levels of intimacy in social life which the documentation of that age rarely illumines. Where you lived, how you dressed, along which streets you walked, where you shopped or bathed or disposed of domestic refuse, your language and gestures, what food you ate and how you prepared it, the pets you kept, how you brought up your children, what expletives you might use in anger ... All of these gave off signals indicative of cultural allegiance, indicative therefore of frontiers which might or might not be negotiable, thresholds which needed to be approached, if at all, with wariness.

Sexual relations were the most intimate of all levels of contact and potentially the most explosive. They have been investigated with subtlety and sensitivity in a recent study by David Nirenberg based on the abundant archival sources surviving in the territories of the Crown of Aragon (the only area in the Mediterranean world where the documentation does light up those otherwise obscure interactions). In Daroca, a small town in Aragon, in 1311, it was rumoured that a Christian girl named Prima Garsón was having an affair with a Muslim neighbour named 'Alī. Terrified, Prima fled. 'Alī was burned at the stake. When Prima was finally tracked down, a medical examination established that she was a virgin. Prima was therefore innocent; so too the unfortunate 'Alī. It's not a pretty story. Prima fled in terror because by law *both* parties to a sexual relationship between a Muslim man and a Christian woman were liable to the death penalty. In relationships between a Christian male and a Muslim female, though the man might suffer disapproval, it was the woman who was punished: law decreed the death penalty, but it was usually commuted to enslavement. (Sex with slaves, incidentally, was permissible and frequent among all three faiths throughout the Mediterranean world.) Enslavement was profitable both for the Crown, who could sell the slave, and for the accusers, who were rewarded with a proportion of the sale price. For the condemned woman the only way of escape was by conversion to Christianity. A case from 1356 reveals the sort of abuse – in every sense – that could arise. It was discovered that the monks (no less) of Roda were sleeping with Muslim women, then shopping them to the authorities for illicit sex so that they were enslaved, and then under privilege from the Crown keeping them either for their further gratification or for sale.

Islamic opinion supported Christian law. In 1347 the Mudejars of Valencia petitioned the king to confirm the penalty of death without the option of monetary compensation for Muslim women found guilty of sexual intercourse with non-Muslims. Transgressing sexual frontiers stained not only the honour of the woman's family but the collective honour of the local Muslim community as a whole. Ysa Yabir of Segovia, author of a book of instruction for Spanish Muslims in the fifteenth century, was categorical in prohibition: 'Whether men or women, they shall not sleep with nor marry infidels.'[4] It was a matter of religious allegiance, not one of race. There is plenty of historical evidence for the marriage of Christian men to women, formerly Muslim, who had converted to Christianity, to set alongside the literary evidence of such works as *Digenes Akrites*. This was so even at the very highest levels. One of the wives of the much-married Alfonso VI of Castile (1065–1109) was the princess Zaida, widow of a governor of Córdoba whose father was the most powerful among the rulers of the *taifa* states, the Emir al-Mu'tamid of Seville (1069–91). Their son Sancho would have succeeded his father on the throne of Castile had he not been killed at the disastrous Battle of Uclés in 1108.

Convivencia was always tense, never relaxed. Whether in Outremer, Sicily or Spain, Muslim and Christian lived side by side, but did not blend. These were multicultural societies only in the severely limited sense that peoples of different culture shared the same territories. Multicultural in the sense of integrated, as the term is usually understood today, they were emphatically not. Nor did they ever seek to be. Multiculturalism as a desirable good would have been incomprehensible to the likes of King Sancho IV or Ysa Yabir or the townsfolk of Daroca who burnt to death the luckless and innocent 'Alī.

In the long term the most fruitful zone of interaction between Christian and Muslim during the crusading epoch lay in intellectual life. As we saw in Chapter 2, a major cultural development of the early Abbasid period was the acquisition by the Islamic scholarly community of the scientific and philosophical learning of the ancient world by means of the translation of its textual heritage into Arabic. We glanced at the diffusion of that corpus of knowledge throughout the

Dār al-Islām, and then at the dawnings, in the mathematical interests of Gerbert of Aurillac, of an awareness that Western scholars had much to learn from their Muslim neighbours. During the twelfth and thirteenth centuries this Arabic corpus was translated into Latin, the language of learning in western Christendom, and thus made available to scholars. This was a process whose significance in the intellectual history of the world it would be hard to exaggerate.

Let us take by way of example Adelard of Bath, who has recently been described as 'the first English scientist'.[5] Adelard, who lived between *c.* 1080 and *c.* 1150, travelled widely in the cultural marchlands of Sicily and Syria for seven years in the early part of the twelfth century. At one time it was thought that he also visited Spain, but modern scholarship has cast doubt on this. (His career is ill documented in detail. One of its few fixed points is this: we know that he was at Mamistra, modern Misis, near Adana in the south-east of today's Turkey, in November 1114 when the region was shaken by an earthquake; the bridge at Misis which Adelard saw shuddering on that occasion still stands.) During these travels Adelard acquired books and also, presumably, the knowledge of Arabic which would enable him to translate them. His works comprised two translations from the Arabic, as well as original compositions of his own which display a debt to Arabic learning. His translation of the Arabic version of Euclid's *Elements* introduced Latin Christendom to the most influential handbook of geometry ever written, one which would become the standard teaching text in the West for the next eight centuries. His translation of the *Zijj*, or astronomical tables, of al-Khwārizmī (d.840), revised by Maslama al-Madjriti ('of Madrid'; d.1007) rendered accessible the most up-to-date astronomical reference book then available. In addition to translations Adelard composed a textbook on the abacus, a treatise on the care of falcons, and a work explaining the use of the astrolabe written for Prince Henry, later to become King Henry II of England (1154–89). Adelard also interested himself in astrology – then widely regarded as an exact science – and cast ten horoscopes for members of the English royal family towards the end of his life. The texts of these predictions survive, written out in what is apparently Adelard's own hand, in a manuscript in the British Library.

Adelard's career is an arresting one in all sorts of ways, not least in its demonstration of the links between knowledge and power. The fragmentary records of his life hint at distinguished connections after his return from his travels, and the work that he was doing in later life suggests that he then held a position as astrologer to the royal court. If so Adelard, as charged with the job of telling his ruler what was going to happen next and even what he ought to do about it, was a very important person indeed, a policy adviser at the highest level. Opportunities of this sort may have been not the least among the attractions of exotic learning in the twelfth and thirteenth centuries.

Adelard stands at the beginning of a period of intense translating activity from both Arabic and Greek into Latin, as a result of which a veritable cornucopia of knowledge was poured out for the enlightenment of Western scholars. Most of this activity occurred in Spain and Italy; a very modest amount in Outremer. In Italy the tendency was for scholars to translate directly from Greek into Latin: thus, for example, James of Venice, a contemporary of Adelard, translated many of Aristotle's scientific works. In Spain translation was mainly of Arabic works, including Arabic renderings of

Greek works. The disadvantage of being at least one remove from the original text was compensated by the accretion of commentary and amplification furnished by intervening Muslim scholars. Thus for example the Irish scholar Michael Scot translated Aristotle's writings *On Animals* in Toledo in about 1216 together with the commentary on them of Ibn Sīnā (or Avicenna: see Chapter 2).

There was nothing planned about this great enterprise, just as there had been nothing planned about the earlier phase of transmission from Greek into Arabic. Inevitably, therefore, work was duplicated. Ptolemy's *Almagest*, the most important astronomical treatise of antiquity, was translated from Greek into Latin by an unknown writer who worked in Sicily in about 1160. At about the same time the prolific translator Gerard of Cremona was translating it from Arabic into Latin in Toledo. Neither scholar had any means of finding out what the other was engaged upon. Inevitably too, work was of very variable quality. Michael Scot's translation of Aristotle's *Animals* was rather slapdash, concerned to convey the general sense of a passage. A generation later, in about 1260, another scholar, the Flemish Dominican William of Moerbeke, did the job again. William's translation, directly from the original Greek, was more careful; a precise and literal rendering.

Known working methods may have been such as to encourage imprecision. A pupil of Gerard of Cremona, the Englishman Daniel of Morley who was active as a translator in Toledo between 1180 and 1200, has left us a description of his master's methods. Gerard had an assistant, Ghalib the Mozarab, who would render the Arabic text verbally into the vernacular, i.e. early Castilian Spanish, and Gerard would then translate it from the vernacular into Latin and write it down. In the instance of Ptolemy's *Almagest*, therefore, the chain of transmission was a long one: Greek into Syriac; Syriac into Arabic (under Barmakid patronage, as we saw in Chapter 2); Arabic verbally into Spanish, to a native of Italy; and Spanish as understood by an Italian into Latin. There was plentiful scope for error, even before we come on to the further scope for error in the copying of texts by hand.

Gerard of Cremona was the most prolific of all the translators. During a sojourn in Toledo of nearly fifty years, from *c.* 1140 until his death in 1187, he translated, according to the latest scholarly estimates, at least eighty-eight works from Arabic into Latin. How did he and other such scholars support themselves? Too often we simply do not know. We have no idea, for example, how Adelard of Bath financed his travels in Italy and Syria. Patronage was an indispensable factor, in an era before, though not long before, the emergence of universities and the academic profession. Michael Scot benefited from the successive patronage of the archbishop of Toledo and the Emperor Frederick II. Archiepiscopal patronage seems to have sustained Gerard of Cremona too, for he is probably to be identified with the 'Master Gerald' who held a canonry in the cathedral of Toledo in the second half of the twelfth century. Royal patronage seems to have assisted Adelard of Bath in later life. English rulers, however, were niggardly patrons of learning by comparison with some of their continental counterparts. Alfonso X of Castile (1252–84) assembled a team of scholars who produced works in the vernacular dependent to varying degrees upon translations from the Arabic: encyclopedias of astronomy and astrology, an illustrated account of chess and other games, a guide to precious stones and their medicinal or magical properties, and more besides. The example of Alfonso X is a reminder that kings could and did commission original works as well as translations. Roger II of Sicily (1130–54) commissioned the Tunisian scholar al-Idrīsī to produce a majestic work of geography flatteringly entitled the *Kitāb ar-Rūjarī* or 'Book of Roger'. The author had a terrestrial globe of silver made to accompany his book, an early example of interactive illustration. The book survives; the globe, sadly, has perished. Frederick II commissioned, and in part himself composed, the greatest book on falconry ever written, the *De Arte Venandi cum Avibus* [The Art of Hunting with Hawks]. Patronage was forthcoming not just because it was part of a ruler's glory to encourage learning but also because the translators were delivering what the age demanded. Consider Gerard's oeuvre. Over half of the works he translated dealt with the mathematical, astronomical and related sciences; about a third with medicine; the remainder with philosophy and logic. These were the branches of knowledge which underpinned the so-called renaissance of the twelfth and thirteenth centuries.

If we take our stand a century or so after Adelard's day we can get a sense of the abundant intellectual harvest that had been gathered in. The range of Greek or Arab authors now available to scholars such as Robert Grosseteste, Bishop of Lincoln (d. 1253), or his pupil Roger Bacon (d. 1292) would have astounded the learned men of Adelard's day. So would the institutions in which they could be studied. Learning had moved away from the monasteries, with their deeply conservative loyalty to a syllabus of study almost exclusively concerned with the Bible and the Church Fathers. The scholars of the thirteenth century studied and argued in new institutions called 'universities' – at Paris, Bologna,

Oxford, to name but three – with libraries, lecture halls and textbooks. The whole atmosphere of scholarship had changed. In this as in many other respects the thirteenth century is recognizably a part of our modern world.

Simply to list names can be tedious, so here instead are three examples of disciplines which were nourished by the new learning. We start with theology. The three related monotheisms of Judaism, Christianity and Islam are 're-vealed' religions. They rest upon divine revelations granted to humankind and recorded in sacred scriptures. The recovery of the Greek thought of antiquity, and especially of the works of Aristotle, presented a challenge. Here was a philosophical system which claimed that the world was intelligible without revelation. The toolkit of reason was all that was required: observation, measurement, logical inference, demonstrable causes and effects. Two contemporaries, one Jewish and the other Muslim, set themselves to confront these disquieting questions. Rabbi Moses Maimonides (1138–1204), a native of Spain but later in life domiciled in Egypt, offered an answer in his *Guide for the Perplexed*. Averroës (1126–98) offered his answer in the form of commentaries upon Aristotle as well as in a number of treatises of his own composition, one of which bore the significant title *On the Harmony of Religion and Philosophy*. A Christian answer necessarily came later, after Maimonides and Averroës had been translated into Latin and absorbed. The most acute and authoritative treatment of the problem was offered by (St) Thomas Aquinas (c.1225–74), whose resolution of the conflicting claims of reason and revelation came to be regarded as normative in Catholic Christendom. In the course of his work Aquinas cited Averroës more frequently than any other non-Christian thinker. Among Western scholars Averroës' commentaries upon Aristotle were so highly regarded that he became known simply as 'the Commentator'. So, for example, Dante could characterize him as '*Averrois che il gran commento feo*' ('Averroës who composed the celebrated commentary': *Inferno* iv. 144), and place him in the select band of non-Christian intellectuals among whom was also to be found, as we saw in Chapter 3, the improbable figure of Saladin.

Second, medicine, about Western knowledge of which Usāmah ibn Munqidh had been so scathing in the twelfth century. Had he been writing two centuries later he might have changed his tune. The story begins at the Benedictine monastery of Monte Cassino in southern Italy, where in the middle years of the eleventh century an inmate named Constantine 'the African' (because he was an immigrant from Tunisia) started to translate medical works from Arabic into Latin because, in his own words, 'among Latin books I could find no author who gave certain or reliable information'.[6] This activity continued in the twelfth century in both Italy and Spain, where the indefatigable Gerard of Cremona translated Avicenna's *Canon* (see Chapter 2) and some two dozen other medical works. Averroës' *Kulliyat* was added to the Latin corpus in the thirteenth century alongside several other works. By about 1300 a very considerable body of Greek and Arabic writings on medicine was available in Latin. They dealt with broadly defined medical sciences, from catalogues of medicinal drugs to practical treatises on surgery or uroscopy. Schools of medicine existed, the most famous of them at Montpellier, where these texts might be studied and skills learnt by aspiring practitioners. The harvest of this activity may be seen in the career and milieu of Arnold (or Arnau in his native Catalan) of Vilanova. Arnold was studying at

Montpellier in the 1260s, and remained connected with its medical school throughout his working life. In 1309 he was the principal adviser behind the papal statutes which regulated the syllabus of studies there. Montpellier was at this epoch politically subject to the Aragonese crown, and this furnished Arnold with the opportunity for advancement. By 1281 he had been appointed personal physician to Peter III of Aragon (1276–85), a position which he retained intermittently (until his death by shipwreck in 1311) under Peter's sons Alfonso III (1285–91) and James II (1291–1327). King James II offers the treat for the historian of the combination of a royal hypochondriac and abundant surviving documentation relating to his personal life. Arnold spent much of his life journeying between the royal court and his teaching and research at Montpellier. In 1297, for example, at the King's request he resided at Barcelona to attend Queen Blanche throughout her second pregnancy.

Arnold was a prolific author. He translated medical works by Galen and Avicenna from Arabic into Latin. He composed a medical handbook for the querulous James II, the *Regimen sanitatis ad inclitum regem Aragonum* [Rule of health for the illustrious King of Aragon], and a tract on military hygiene on the occasion of the King's campaign against Almería in 1309. He wrote an elaborate treatise on medical theory, the *Speculum Medicine* [The Mirror of Medicine]. He also wrote on non-medical matters. His works on eschatology such as *De Adventu Antichristi* [On the Coming of Antichrist] attracted accusations of heresy, while his pamphlets calling for reform of the Church angered clerical conservatives. But he had friends in high places to protect him, among them no less a person than Pope Boniface VIII (whom he cured of a painful kidney stone in 1301), though the Pope did sigh over what he saw as Arnold's wilfulness: 'If only you would occupy yourself with medicine and leave theology alone, we could honour you!'[7] Arnold assembled a considerable library. Over a hundred books were inventoried shortly after his death – a very large number for a private collector at that period – of which about a third could be classified as medical or scientific. They constitute a roll-call of the medical literature available in Latin, original works and translations, in Arnold's day.

Arnold of Vilanova was a remarkable scholar and practitioner. Recent research has shown that he needs to be considered against a backdrop of thriving medical activity in the various western Mediterranean territories which made up the Aragonese federation, and especially in its big cities such as Barcelona and Valencia. Medical practitioners, at various levels from apothecaries to surgeons, were numerous. Their training was steadily improving. They had a strong sense of collective identity and professional pride, and a recognized and valued social role. None of this could have come about without the translating activity of the previous two centuries.

My final example hardly deserves the name of a discipline. Rather, we should think of it as a programme of enquiry, loosely linked to medical study, hesitant at first but gaining confidence and stamina by the early part of the fourteenth century. It has only recently been delineated and investigated, for the first time, in a ground-breaking study by Peter Biller entitled *The Measure of Multitude*: *Population in medieval thought*. This programme or zone of enquiry embodied the development of disciplined thinking about population: size, distribution, sex-ratio, marriage and procreation, birth control, disease, mortality, and so forth. The author convincingly

shows how medieval thought about population was encouraged and shaped first by scientific translations from the Greek
(especially Aristotle) and Arabic (especially Avicenna and
Averroës), and secondly by contemplation of the juxtaposition of Christendom with what was believed about the
Islamic world or the worlds beyond it revealed by the envoys
to the Mongols in the thirteenth century. The implications
of incipient demographic thought were considerable. Just as
the advances in medical knowledge and practice encouraged
a view of bodily infirmity as something that could be
observed and to a degree corrected, so thought about population would in time open vistas of thinking about human
society not as God-given but as manipulable.

Intellectual interchange relating to *religious* culture – as
opposed to philosophical or scientific – has a rather different
tale to tell. There is still strikingly little sign that the learned
men of Islam displayed any interest in Christianity as such.
Perhaps this is not surprising. The revelation vouchsafed to
the Prophet superseded the partial revelations granted to
earlier prophets such as Moses or Jesus. There could be
no incentive to study the tenets of faiths which had been
overtaken and rendered redundant by the fullness of God's
revelation. The only occasion for doing so, accordingly, was
for the purpose of engaging in polemic. Thus, for example,
al-Ṭabarī used his knowledge of Christianity in composing
his apologetic work in defence of Islam in ninth-century
Baghdad (see Chapter 2).

Ibn Ḥazm of Córdoba (994–1064) has been claimed as an
exception to this pattern. Distinguished as a jurist, philosopher and poet, in the present context Ibn Ḥazm's most
striking work was his *Kitāb al-Fasl*, its full title literally
translated as 'The Book of the Distinction in the Religious

Heresies and Sects', usually known for convenience as 'The Book of Sects'. In it Ibn Ḥazm set himself to proclaim and defend the rightness of Islam against all other faiths and deviations from Islam: a devout act of *jihād*. This involved refuting the claims of Christianity. In doing so Ibn Ḥazm demonstrated a remarkably detailed knowledge of Christian sacred texts, presumably acquired by reading the Arabic translations of the Bible used by the Mozarabic Christians of al-Andalus which he could have procured without difficulty in Córdoba. Some modern scholars have seen in Ibn Ḥazm's work an early essay in 'comparative religion' or 'inter-faith dialogue'. But this is wholly misleading. Ibn Ḥazm needed to know about Christianity for the sole end of refuting it, which he judged accomplished by pedantic exposure of textual inconsistency. For example, pouncing upon the biblical passages which assert that John the Baptist neither ate nor drank (Matthew 11: 18) and that he lived off locusts and wild honey (Mark 1: 6), Ibn Ḥazm triumphantly proclaimed,

In this passage there is lying and contradiction . . . one of the two reports is a lie without a doubt . . . All this shows that the Christian community is altogether vile.[8]

This is not the language of anything that we may reckon as dialogue. Ibn Ḥazm's cast of mind was hostile to Christianity from the outset. *The Book of Sects* may have been learned; it was in no way tolerant.

These attitudes on the Islamic side of the religio-cultural divide were precisely matched on the Christian. The writings of John of Damascus at which we glanced briefly in Chapter 1, the *Dialogue* and *On Heresies*, especially the latter, offer parallels with the work of Ibn Ḥazm. John ridiculed the heresy of the Ishmaelites in the eighth century in much the same way as Ibn Ḥazm was to mock the sect of the Christians in the eleventh.

We encounter the same attitudes when we move on into the twelfth century. Here the most celebrated episode is the first translation of the Koran into Latin. This ambitious intellectual operation was commissioned by Peter the Venerable, abbot of the famous Benedictine monastery of Cluny, in Burgundy, in the course of a visitation of Cluny's Spanish daughter-houses in the year 1142. For this task Abbot Peter engaged two scholars whom he met in Spain, the Englishman Robert of Ketton and the German Hermann of Carinthia, who had gone there to translate scientific works from Arabic into Latin. Subsidiary members of the team were Master Peter of Toledo, probably drawn from the Toledan Mozarabic community; Peter of Poitiers, the abbot's secretary; and a Muslim named Muhammad the Saracen, otherwise unidentifiable. Robert was responsible for the translation of the Koran, which he completed within a very short time, having regard to the length and linguistic complexity of the text, by about midsummer 1143. This project, like Ibn Ḥazm's, has been hailed by some modern historians as an episode of enlightenment and toleration. In reality it was nothing of the kind. Robert's translation of the Koran was accompanied by marginal glosses conceived in a hostile and nit-picking spirit. Consider, for example, the following: 'And We gave David bounty from Us . . . and we softened for him iron: "fashion wide coats of mail, and measure well the links"' (Koran 34:10). The glossator commented on this as follows:

The madman claims that David was the first to find out the technique of fashioning chain-mail; but it is recorded in holy scripture that Goliath whom that same David slew while he was still a boy was clad in mail![9]

It is likely that the negative spirit of these annotations reflects guidelines laid down by Abbot Peter himself. So much is suggested by the use Peter made of the newly-translated Koran, which was to compose a work of polemic whose tone is indicated by its title: *A Book against the Abominable Heresy or Sect of the Saracens*. Like Ibn Ḥazm a century beforehand, Abbot Peter of Cluny needed his texts not for the purpose of engaging in dialogue but in order to score points off and to refute his enemy. His mind, too, was already made up.

Robert of Ketton's translation of the Koran was quickly forgotten. The manuscript gathered dust in Cluny's library until it was rediscovered and printed in the sixteenth century. When a canon of Toledo named Mark undertook a translation of the Koran early in the thirteenth century he thought that he was doing something that no one had done before, so completely had all memory of Abbot Peter's enterprise perished. Mark's translation was more literal and precise than Robert of Ketton's; a better aid to the understanding of Islam's sacred text. It was commissioned by the archbishop of Toledo, Rodrigo Ximénez de Rada (whom we have already met as the patron of Michael Scot). This commission should be seen in the wider context of Archbishop Rodrigo's literary work, which included among much else a *Historia Arabum* [History of the Arabs], a brief survey of Islamic history from its origins down to the middle years of the twelfth century.

Archbishop Rodrigo's work was but one of several from the thirteenth century which displayed a knowledge of

Islamic history and doctrine. Some of these works display also a new feature, briefly alluded to at the end of Chapter 3: the first hints of the notion of religious pluralism. Consider Rodrigo's contemporary William of Auvergne – academic, preacher, pastoral moralist, and from 1228 until his death in 1249, bishop of Paris. When William wrote about Islam or about Judaism he chose words – indeed, he sometimes created words, such as *Saracenismus*, 'Saracenism' – which indicated precisely a sense of a people and their religious culture which were different from those of Christendom. If Islam were becoming in Christian eyes a culture inviting study and understanding, rather than something to be swept under the carpet as an aberrant form of Christianity, or mocked as an absurd farrago of contradictions, that would register a very considerable intellectual advance. The first steps in that direction were taken in the thirteenth century.

5

Sieving the Koran

The loss in 1291 of Acre, last outpost of Outremer, did not
signal the end of crusading. Far from it: the urge to regain
the Holy Places of Christendom remained as strong as ever.
Dante embodied the spirit of the early fourteenth-century
age in his *Divina Commedia*. The warrior saints whom he
encountered in Paradise included those who had won renown
in battle with the Saracens such as Roland who fell at Roncesvalles or Godfrey de Bouillon who had conquered Jerusalem
in 1099. The half century or so which followed the loss of
Acre was notable for the number of crusading projects which
were touted round papal and royal courts in an attempt to
get the leaders of Christendom to sponsor further crusades.
The most ambitious of these was the brainchild of a Venetian,
Marino Sanudo, a relative of the Sanudo dukes of Archipelago mentioned in the previous chapter, who presented his
plans to Pope John XXII in 1321 in the form of a substantial
book entitled *Liber Secretorum Fidelium Crucis* [The Book
of the Secrets of the Faithful of the Cross]. They were care-
fully thought out. An economic blockade of the Nile Delta
would be followed by the sending in of an international task
force to secure Egypt, after which the main crusading army
would advance upon Jerusalem overland. No detail escaped

Sanudo's attention. Recruitment, training, weapons, shipping, victualling, costing – all were there. Sanudo spent the next twenty years seeking sponsors, tirelessly lobbying, travelling, organizing conferences, writing letters – and in the process, one suspects, becoming a bit of a bore – but all to no avail. When he died in 1343 he stipulated in his will that his writings should always be available for consultation. It was the heartfelt plea of a disappointed man.

Another dossier of crusading plans was presented to Edward III of England in about 1330 by a Yorkshire gentleman named Roger of Stonegrave. Roger had had an eventful career. As a young man he had joined the military order of the Hospitallers and had been sent out to assist in the defence of what was left of Outremer. Captured at Acre in 1291, he seems to have spent the next eighteen years, no less, as a prisoner-of-war in Egypt. He used his long captivity wisely, observing much and remembering it. Released after the Hospitallers acquired the island of Rhodes in 1309, Roger finally made his way back to Yorkshire in 1318, where he took up his pen. The plans he submitted to the King were in many ways akin to Sanudo's; what Roger could distinctively contribute was an exceptionally detailed and accurate knowledge of Egypt under the rule of the Mamlūk sultans.

Some of these schemes had an engagingly eccentric quality. A French lawyer, Pierre Dubois, composed in about 1306 a work entitled *De Recuperatione Terrae Sanctae* [On the Recovery of the Holy Land], which he presented to King Philip IV. For the most part as serious and sober as the writings of Sanudo or Roger of Stonegrave, at one point an element of sheer fantasy breaks through. Dubois proposed to educate personable young women in Western Europe who might then be shipped out to the Levant to captivate and marry Greek Christians, convert them to Latin or Roman observance, and thus facilitate the formation of a united front in the face of Islam. The king of France's reaction is not recorded.

The popes and monarchs who were the targets of all this crusade propaganda in the early fourteenth century never did get an expedition together for the repossession of the Holy Land. It was not that there was any lack of will. One of the many revelations of recent study of the Crusades is that the crusading ideal was not 'in decline', as historians used to assert, after a high point in the age of Richard the Lionheart or St Louis. The desire to undertake crusades remained as strong and as unquestioned in later medieval Europe as ever it had been. What repeatedly thwarted the realization of crusading plans was the state of international relations within western Christendom. The most powerful monarchy in the West was that of France; and by tradition her kings felt a sincere and special duty towards the crusade. But from the latter part of the thirteenth century onwards the kings of France were engaged in those long drawn-out, intermittent and debilitating hostilities with England which modern historians misleadingly call the Hundred Years' War. Their hands were tied: they could not emulate their revered predecessor Louis IX and abandon their realm to go crusading in Egypt and Syria for years at a stretch.

This does not mean that no crusading expeditions took place, simply that those which did occur tended to be small-scale operations with limited objectives. In 1344, for example, a squadron of only about three dozen ships provided by the Venetians, Pope Clement VI and the Hospitallers of Rhodes managed to capture the important harbour of Smyrna, on the western coast of Asia Minor. The Hospitallers held it until

1402. Another instance is furnished by King Peter I of Cyprus (1359–69), a member of the French Lusignan dynasty which had ruled the island as a sort of offshore Outremer since the time of the Third Crusade. After travelling widely in Western Europe to recruit troops and gain papal sponsorship, in 1365 he led an expedition which sacked and plundered Alexandria but did not establish any permanent base there.

A final, and very different, example of fourteenth-century crusading is provided by the Crusade of Nicopolis. But Nicopolis (now Nikopol) is on the Danube, on the northern frontier of today's Bulgaria. What on earth was a crusading expedition doing there? To answer that question we must go back to Asia Minor. The disintegration of what was left of the sultanate of the Seljuk Turks (see Chapter 3) in the face of the Mongol advance had left a power vacuum in Asia Minor. This was filled initially – as in Syria or al-Andalus in the eleventh century – by a number of small and quarrelsome principalities. One of the more westerly among these was established in the early fourteenth century by an immigrant Turkish tribal leader named Osman – from whom the name Ottoman is mis-derived – in the hilly country to the south of the Sea of Marmara round the modern town of Bursa. Osman died in 1326. During the next seventy years Ottoman suzerainty was expanded over most of mainland Asia Minor. It was extended also into south-eastern or Balkan Europe, an area once part of the Byzantine Empire. That empire, however, had been fatally weakened by the disastrous events of the Fourth Crusade (see Chapter 3). The restoration of the empire-in-exile at Nicaea to Constantinople in 1261 installed there a polity that was a shadow of what it had once been. For the last two centuries of its existence the region of direct imperial rule was effectively confined to the city of Constantinople and a steadily shrinking territorial hinterland nearby.

The Ottomans' self-image was as *ghāzīs*, frontiersmen on the edge of the *Dār al-Islām* whose duty it was to extend the scope of the faith by *jihād*. Using diplomacy as well as war, their advance into Europe seemed unstoppable. From an initial bridgehead at Gallipoli in 1354 they fanned out to establish lordship over, and subsequently direct rule in, Bulgaria, Serbia, Albania and northern Greece, winning a series of victories over the local principalities among which that at Kosovo in 1389 was the most celebrated. By the 1390s Ottoman dominion in Europe stretched from the Danube and the Black Sea right down to Thessaly (now in Northern Greece).

This was the background to the Crusade of Nicopolis in 1396. This crusading expedition was different from others of its day in that it was neither limited in its objectives nor small in its scale. Its aim was nothing less than to halt the advance of the Ottoman Turks. An international force was recruited in France, Germany and England to form what was quite possibly the biggest crusading army ever assembled, which then marched down the Danube under the leadership of King Sigismund of Hungary. Meanwhile a fleet under the command of the Grand Master of the Hospitallers and containing ships from both Genoa and Venice (in one of their rare moments of collaboration) made its way into the Black Sea and up the Danube to join forces with the crusading army. The land and sea forces settled down to besiege the strategically important town of Nicopolis. But there they were surprised by a relieving Turkish army and catastrophically defeated. The most ambitious crusading venture of the later Middle Ages had ended in a humiliating defeat.

The setback at Nicopolis left Constantinople vulnerable.

It is probable that the city would have fallen swiftly to Turkish assault had the Ottomans not been attacked in their rear by a new Mongol aggressor. This was 'Tīmūr the Lame', better remembered in the West as Tamerlane or Tamburlaine. Tamerlane's western campaign of 1402 was but a minor pendant to his Central Asian conquests and his Chinese ambitions. But it matters for our story because in the course of it he inflicted a serious defeat on the Ottomans – Sultan Bāyazīd I was captured, and died in captivity – devastated much of their Asia Minor heartlands, and, almost incidentally, put an end to Hospitaller dominion in Smyrna. Tamerlane's campaign against the Ottomans gave Constantinople a breathing space.

The respite did not last for long. Sultan Muhammad II (1451–81) had on his own admission been possessed since childhood by a desire to conquer the city of Constantine. He was obsessed by the memory of Alexander the Great, whose deeds as recorded by Arrian were read to him daily. So strong was the Sultan's sense of identification with Alexander that he even went so far as to commission an account of his own deeds, in Greek, to be copied on the same paper and in the same format as his own copy of Arrian's biography of Alexander, next to which it would be shelved in his library. It was to this ruler that there fell the honour of conquering the city when he was only twenty years old. The last Byzantine emperor, appropriately called Constantine, perished bravely in vain defence of the breached walls. On 29 May 1453 Sultan Muhammad made his formal entry into Constantinople.

The conqueror followed up this triumph by consolidating Ottoman power throughout the Black Sea zone, the Balkans and Greece. From the western outpost of Bosnia raids were launched every year into Croatia, Styria, Carinthia, even northern Italy. In 1477 a raid approached so close to Venice that the flames of Ottoman ravaging were visible from the city. After Muhammad's death the Ottoman assault was stayed for a generation or so. Under Sulaimān I, 'the Magnificent' (1520–66), it was renewed. Belgrade was conquered in 1521. The Hungarians were defeated at Mohács in 1526 and the eastern part of their kingdom passed under Turkish control. Vienna itself was besieged in 1529. Wallachia, Transylvania and Moldovia became tributaries. Meanwhile, in the south-east, the Ottomans had brought Mamlūk rule in Egypt, western Arabia and Syria to an end in 1517 and brought these provinces too under their control. Western Christendom, divided as never before by the stresses of the Reformation, was now confronted by a formidable and hostile Ottoman Empire that stretched from Hungary to Libya.

In some respects the fifteenth-century Ottoman advance resembles the initial expansion of Islam eight centuries beforehand. People of the Book continued to receive toleration. Within months of the fall of Constantinople a deal had been struck between the Sultan and Patriarch Gennadios. The Ottomans would protect the Greek ecclesiastical establishment – not least against Christian rivals such as the Serbian Orthodox Church. The Patriarch would guarantee Greek civil loyalty and prevent any Greek intrigue with the Ottomans' – and his – Catholic enemies. Privately the Patriarch might refer to the Turks as 'bloody dogs of Hagar';[1] in practice the arrangement proved convenient to both parties, though difficult times lay ahead. In the capital, Greek Church and people flourished. For most of the Ottoman period, down to the early twentieth century, the population of Constantinople (or Istanbul as we may now begin to call it) was divided in the approximate proportions 60 per cent Muslim to 40 per cent Christian and Jewish. It never became a demographically Islamic city in the sense that, say, Baghdad was.

In the conquered Balkan provinces there was no sweeping replacement of one governing class by another. Christian landowners could, and many did, retain their estates in return for rendering military service as cavalry. The most burdensome levy upon the provinces was the practice known as *devshirme* or 'gathering'. This was the regular conscription of large numbers of Christian boys from the rural population and their deportation to Istanbul where they were given a new Islamic identity and became the servants of the state. The best-known role for these youths was as the *yeni ceri*, meaning 'new troops', anglicized as 'Janissaries', the elite military corps which made Ottoman armies so formidable. But this was not the only role for the 'gathered'. Some rose to high positions in the bureaucracy or other professions. The greatest Ottoman architect of the sixteenth century, embellisher of Istanbul with mosques for Sulaimān the Magnificent, was Sinan the Old – he lived to be about ninety – an Armenian from Anatolia who had been brought to the capital as one of the 'gathered'.

Sinan was prominent among those who helped to turn Istanbul into an architecturally Islamic city – just as had happened to other Christian cities in the past, such as Córdoba. Substantially populated by non-Muslims though it was, its public face was unambiguously Islamic. Soon after the conquest the grave of one of the companions of the Prophet was conveniently (if improbably) discovered at the top of the Golden Horn: it became, and remains today, the most revered Muslim holy place in Turkey. Relics of the Prophet himself were translated from Mecca to Istanbul after the conquest of the Mamlūks in 1517. Mosques and minarets, religious schools, hospitals and almshouses were architectural manifestos of Islamic piety. Rituals such as the *selamlik*, the sultan's formal procession to Friday prayers, conveyed the same message.

Lack of evidence makes it difficult to chart changes of religious allegiance with any confidence in those rural areas which were among the initial conquests of Islam back in the seventh and eighth centuries. With the assistance of a category of document known as a *mufassal defter* we can set our sights a little higher in the Ottoman period. The *defter* was a statistical survey of a given province for fiscal purposes which listed the taxable hearths village by village and also indicated the religious affiliations of each household. Surveys of this type conducted in the 1520s reveal interesting contrasts. In rural Anatolia, the central tableland of Asia Minor, Muslim households numbered 92 per cent of the taxable whole, Christian ones a mere 8 per cent. In the Balkan provinces at the same date, Muslim households constituted 19 per cent, as against 81 per cent Christian ones. Why this contrast? In Anatolia there had been an Islamic presence since the first coming of the Seljuks more than four centuries before. For much of this period there had been serious economic and social dislocation in Anatolia caused by the passing and repassing of armies, migrants, refugees and slavers. Christians had tended to migrate to the coastal strips, such as Trebizond and its neighbourhood, where a continuing Byzantine imperial presence offered some protection. On the Anatolian plateau Christianity withered and eventually died, somewhat as it had done in North Africa. In the Balkans, by contrast, the Ottoman presence was relatively recent, the conquest had been swift and centrally directed, the ensuing disruption less destabilizing than in Anatolia. Christian communities were evidently thriving there in the sixteenth century, and would continue to do so. Their situation was not unlike that of the Mozarabs of Spain.

If we turn now to Spain, we find that a completely different balance of forces was coming into being as eastern Europe was being overrun by the Ottomans. The only independent Muslim principality left in the Iberian Peninsula by the late thirteenth century was the emirate of Granada. This did not mean that Christian monarchs could relax their vigilance. The rise of a new power among the turbulent and zealous Muslims of the Maghrib might threaten the Christian states with invasion in concert with the emir of Granada. This happened in 1340 when the Merinids – successors to the Almohads in Morocco – crossed the Straits and joined forces with Granada to mount an invasion of Castile. They were defeated decisively at the Battle of the Rio Salado. Thereafter the military danger to the Christian kings diminished, though it did not disappear. Their security was enhanced by the Castilian capture of Algeciras in 1344, which yielded a measure of control over the Straits, and was reinforced by later conquests, such as the Portuguese acquisition of Ceuta in 1415.

After the mid fourteenth century the emirate of Granada survived on sufferance as a tributary of the kingdom of Castile. It was only the civil strife that engulfed Christian Spain for much of the ensuing century that enabled its emirs to preserve a fragile independence. (To that strife therefore we owe, indirectly, the Alhambra.) In 1469 the dynastic marriage of two heirs-apparent, Isabella of Castile and Ferdinand of Aragon, brought into prospect the union of the two principal peninsular monarchies, which was realized in 1474.

From 1482 the war for Granada was waged in earnest. Like his contemporary Muhammad II, Ferdinand thought of himself as a man of destiny – or at any rate encouraged his propagandists to present him in this light. What Constantinople was to the Ottoman sultan, Granada was to Ferdinand and Isabella. They accomplished their desire. On 2 January 1492 they received the keys of the city from its last Muslim ruler.

The war for Granada was in the technical, legal sense a crusade. Crusading zeal remained lively in the fifteenth century. Philip the Good, Duke of Burgundy (1419–67) – whose father had been captured at Nicopolis in the year of his son's birth – proclaimed until the end of his life his earnest desire to crusade against the Turks. Pope Pius II (1458–64) died at Ancona on the eastern coast of Italy while leading in person what he hoped, vainly, would be a crusade to recover Constantinople. Prince Henry 'the Navigator', of the royal family of Portugal, believed that the horoscope cast for him by a court astrologer at the time of his birth in 1394 showed that he was destined to accomplish 'great and noble conquests' as a crusader.[2] In his will he put it on record that he had been dedicated by his parents at birth to the crusader-king St Louis IX of France. The Ceuta campaign of 1415, which Henry led, was seen by him as a crusade. The exploration which he sponsored down Africa's Atlantic coast was undertaken not primarily out of geographical curiosity, but in a spirit of Christian assertion – and also for self-enrichment. (As it happened, Islam was becoming more widespread and robust in West African kingdoms such as Mali in the fourteenth century and Songhay in the fifteenth, though how far Henry and his advisers were aware of this is not certain.)

The crusading ideal, then, remained powerful in later medieval Christendom, whether its fruits were defeat at Nicopolis or victory at Granada. Defeat could be explained away. Among the anguished heart-searchings of the post-Nicopolis years was a poem by Honorat Bouvet, a Provençal monk, diplomat and jurist. Bouvet pointed to the moral shortcomings of Christendom – its profanity, blasphemy, lack of charity, sexual immorality, material self-indulgence – as conduct displeasing to God. How could He give victory to those who were guilty of such sins as these? Nothing new here: clerical moralists had been accounting for crusading failures along these lines ever since St Bernard of Clairvaux had set himself to explain the failure of the Second Crusade back in the twelfth century. What *is* surprising, however, is that in Bouvet's poem the diagnostician who identifies Christendom's shortcomings is not a Christian but a Muslim. Further, some of his diagnosis takes the form of a comparison between Christian and Muslim societies in favour of the latter. For example, wrote Bouvet, self-indulgence in food, drink and clothing has made the Christians go soft; but Muslims are toughened by austerity. Christians are divided, but Muslims – Bouvet's gaze was probably upon the Ottoman Turks alone – have the strength which comes from unity. And there is more along the same lines. Now the literary device of using the outsider as critic, a stick with which to beat your own society, involves thinking neutrally, even benevolently, about that outsider and his views. Bouvet's *Sarrasin* is as sympathetic as the fictional correspondents in Montesquieu's *Lettres persanes* were to be three centuries later. The machinery of his poem seems to presuppose a more well-disposed attitude towards the Muslim 'Other' than we might expect to find in crusading circles.

The point could be put in a slightly different way. There were circles other than crusading ones; approaches to the Islamic world other than the way of military confrontation. One such approach was a missionary one, and to understand this we need to go back in time for a moment. One of the key features of the reform of the Church in the twelfth century was an emphasis on preaching, not just for the instruction of the ignorant, but especially and deliberately for the correction of the deviant. Those who erred and strayed into heresy – and there were beginning to be an alarming number of them around – were to be taught back into the fold by means of sermons. The best-known initiative was that of Domingo (or Dominic), prior of the Castilian bishopric of Osma: in 1220 he founded the preaching order which still bears his name, the Dominican friars. Now this impulse to preach to dissidents soon became focused on the target of the most dangerous and stubborn of all heretics, the Muslims. Domingo's bishop, Diego of Osma, had wanted to resign his see in order to go and preach the Gospel in al-Andalus, and Domingo planned to accompany him. He initially conceived of his Order of Preachers as directed against Islam. It was Pope Innocent III who persuaded him that the new order should rather be targeted against heretics nearer home, the Albigenses or Cathars of southern France.

Missionary work was high on the agenda of thirteenth-century churchmen. This was the age of the Mongol missions, as we saw in Chapter 3. It was also the age in which Christianity was being pressed upon the remaining pagans of northern Europe: the Prussians, Estonians and Finns. It is not surprising, therefore, to find thought being devoted to planning missions to Islam. Take, for example, Ramón de Peña-fort, who resigned his generalship of the Dominican Order in 1240, when in his mid fifties, to devote himself to missions to Muslims. He founded schools for the study of Arabic where missionaries might be trained. His admiring biographer claimed that they made 10,000 converts. We may wish to take this figure with a generous pinch of salt, but need not doubt that the number was considerable. These converts were presumably made in the course of 'internal' missions directed at the Muslims who had come under Christian rule in the course of the territorial expansion of the peninsular monarchies in the thirteenth century. (There were, of course, other forces making for changes in religious allegiance which had nothing to do with such missionary work.) Peñafort's fellow Dominican, Ramón Martí, who was fluent in both Arabic and Hebrew, compiled an Arabic–Latin dictionary for the use of students in these academies. Youngest in this trio of thirteenth-century Catalan Ramóns was the Majorcan polymath Ramón Lull (1232–1315). Lull was a truly remarkable figure: knight, poet, novelist, mystic, traveller, self-publicist, author of over 200 works, and lobbyist as tireless as Sanudo for the causes which he championed. Lull established a college near his home in Majorca for the training of missionaries to Islam. At the Ecumenical Council of Vienne in 1311 he persuaded the assembled churchmen to found schools of oriental studies at the universities of Paris, Oxford, Bologna and Salamanca, in which the Arabic language might be taught, together with the history, theology and philosophy of Islam. He had already shown what might be done in several of his multitudinous works. For example, his *Liber del Gentil e dels Tres Savis* [Book of the Pagan and the Three Sages] of 1277 was an account of meetings between a pagan and a Jew, a Christian and a Muslim, in the course of which the representatives of the three monotheisms put the case for their respective faiths. Lull practised what he preached. On three occasions he went to Tunisia to preach the Gospel. These were the actions of a brave or a foolhardy man: Islamic law prescribes the death penalty for such preaching. On the first two occasions Lull was lucky to get off with spells of imprisonment. On the third occasion he was stoned to death.

Such overt proselytizing was never going to make headway. A more discreet approach lay in the sending of chaplains to Christian communities under Islamic rule, or the establishment of religious orders devoted to ministry among, and the ransoming of, prisoners-of-war and other captives. If their brief was not the conversion of infidels, it was concerned with mission in the more limited sense of sustaining 'expatriate' Christian communities. Two orders devoted to captives came into existence early in the thirteenth century, the Trinitarians and the Mercedarians, both of them open to women as well as men. Over the centuries they did much good work. The most famous prisoner to owe his release to their efforts was Miguel de Cervantes when he lay captive in Algiers in the 1570s.

There could have been no question of attempting to convert the Ottomans to Christianity by mission in the early fifteenth century, and crusading against them had proved a humiliating failure. Moreover, it was at just this time that the ecclesiastical authority most closely identified with both crusade and mission experienced unprecedented humiliation. Dissident theologians such as the grumpy Oxford don John Wycliffe (d.1384) criticized the theoretical bases of papal authority. The Great Schism between 1378 and 1417 offered the unedifying spectacle of two, and for a short time even three, rival claimants to the papacy. The churchmen associated with the so-called Conciliar Movement sought to limit papal authority by subjecting it to the supremacy of a General Council of the Church. Fifteenth-century pronouncements on the justness or otherwise of warfare against non-Christians display a hesitation which would have surprised an earlier generation. These scruples can be sensed, for example, in the very long *consulta*, or legal opinions, on this topic, prepared on papal orders by two eminent Italian canon lawyers in 1436. Former confident certainties seemed to be evaporating.

In these circumstances, with the Turks at the very threshold of western Christendom and Constantinople in her death agony, some new initiative was required. It was found in the favoured intellectual armoury of the age of Renaissance humanism: textual study and rhetoric. First learn about Islam, then argue courteously with its adherents (rather than preach at them). Two figures are representative: the Spaniard John of Segovia (d.1458) and the German Nicholas of Cusa (d.1464). John was a professor of theology at Salamanca who was sent by his university to represent it at the long-running Council of Basle between 1433 and 1449. There he met many of the leading intellectual figures of the day, including Nicholas. In his native land the schools of Arabic studies which Lull and others had founded had long ago decayed. John wanted to revive the study of Islam in Spain, and to this end prepared a new translation of the Koran, a trilingual version in Arabic, Latin and Castilian. (He was assisted in this work by Ysa Yabir of Segovia, whose views on inter-cultural sexual relations were quoted in Chapter 4.) John hoped that on the basis of renewed study Christian intellectuals would be enabled to engage in peaceful dialogue with their Muslim counterparts. The forum which he envisaged for these encounters was to be a prolonged academic conference (perhaps not unlike the Church council in which John spent so large a proportion of his working life). The spirit of discussion he aspired to foster was one which sought points of contact between Christianity and Islam, rather than stressing their differences as earlier controversialists such as Ibn Ḥazm or Peter the Venerable had done. Convergence, not divergence, was to be the watchword; and John was convinced that right-intentioned scholars could talk themselves into it. Sadly, John's high-minded idealism bore no fruit in practice. His offer to engage in conference with the Islamic scholars of Granada was rejected by those threatened men, who by the fifteenth century had withdrawn into a last bastion of intolerant confessional intransigence. His trilingual Koran, bequeathed to his university of Salamanca, was lost by his neglectful fellow professors and has never been found. His pupil Hernando de Talavera, first archbishop of reconquered Granada, tried to put John's ideas into practice in his approaches to his Muslim flock after 1492. But his conciliatory policies were brushed aside by the Archbishop of Toledo and Primate of Spain, Cardinal Cisneros, who insisted upon a policy of forced baptism instead (with disastrous consequences, but that is another story).

Nicholas of Cusa started out an academic like John of Segovia, at Cologne, where he was influenced by his reading of the works of Ramón Lull. But he moved on to a broader career as a diplomat in papal service and an ecclesiastical statesman, which brought him the Tyrolese bishopric of Brixen and a cardinal's hat. Nicholas was a man of astonishing intellectual gifts, distinguished alike as philosopher, theologian, mathematician and historian. His friend Pope Pius II asked Nicholas to write something in support of his crusading plans: he must have been dismayed at what he got. The work, entitled *Cribratio Alcorani* [The Sieving of the Koran], is dedicated to the proposition that if the Koran is intensively studied in the proper spirit ('sieved') it will be found to be compatible with the teachings of Christianity as found in the New Testament. Beneath discrepancies and differences there lay a shared basis of belief. The convergence that John of Segovia sought was there. Nicholas went even further in his most ambitious work, *Docta Ignorantia* [Learned Ignorance]. Its main theme was the inaccessibility to the human intellect of ultimate Truth. Human knowledge can never be more than conjectural or approximate or provisional. Wisdom lies in acknowledging ignorance. If Truth is to be apprehended it can only be by means of mystical intuition. Although Nicholas never asserted this in so many words, he seemed to come close to the view that ways to God existed which were independent of confessional allegiance. If a Christian mystic could find God, could not a Muslim sufi also? Nicholas of Cusa opened up distant and disturbing perspectives which would attract some of the most adventurous minds of Renaissance Europe; they would also prove attractive to a much later age concerned with 'interfaith dialogue'.

The eirenic hopes of such thinkers as John of Segovia and Nicholas of Cusa, building upon the pioneering labours of Lull and his circle, coexisted with the crusading impulses of such as Henry the Navigator and Ferdinand of Aragon. Later medieval attitudes to Islam were more diverse than they had been in the twelfth and thirteenth centuries. Some of the modes of contact remained unchanged. Western demand for eastern luxury commodities was diminished neither by the Ottoman advance nor by Mediterranean piracy, which was on its way to reaching something of a crescendo in the sixteenth century. So merchants continued to ply to and fro, and were encouraged to do so by the conquerors. It was only two days after his formal entry into Constantinople that Muhammad II granted a privilege to the Genoese confirming their status as protected subjects of the Sultan; the Genoese quarter continued to be across the Golden Horn in Galata, as it had been since the twelfth century. The expatriate merchant dynasties of Genoa were enduring. The Testa family, for example, settled in Constantinople in the thirteenth century; they remained there until the twentieth. The English 'port dynasties' of the Douro look like newcomers by comparison.

Other modes of contact were less in evidence in the later Middle Ages than they had been at an earlier date. The break-up of the unitary Mongol Empire made eastward travel overland much more difficult and after the age of Marco Polo there were fewer European travellers to be found on the caravan routes of Central Asia or beyond. It is symbolic, perhaps, that the most widely-travelled adventurer of the fourteenth century was wholly fictional: Sir John Mandeville, whose imaginary and richly enjoyable *Travels* seem to have been composed in about 1360 (their authorship has not yet been convincingly identified). Maritime exploration, of course, was a different matter; but its intent was to leapfrog over the *Dār al-Islām*, not to pass observantly through it.

Intellectual enquiry, outside the circles of such as John of Segovia or Nicholas of Cusa, was another form of contact that slackened. The couple of centuries that elapsed between the lifetime of Adelard of Bath and that of Arnold of Vilanova formed the heroic age of intellectual acquisition. That does not mean that the translation of Arabic or Greek scientific works came to a sudden stop in the early fourteenth century; of course not: but there was less of it thereafter. Among several plausible explanations of this phenomenon, the most cogent is also the simplest. Western Christendom had got all that it needed from the Islamic world. Kick-started by the translators, Western intellectuals could now run on their own. The careers and writings of, say, Arnold himself, or of Roger Bacon, exemplify the point. The scientific advances of the later medieval period were self-generated. To a large degree they were of a technical kind – in cartography, navigation, shipbuilding, clockmaking, gunnery and printing.

Gutenberg's Bible was printed in 1455. By 1500, less than half a century later, there were over 100 towns in western Christendom which housed printing-presses and 6 million volumes or so had been printed. In some cities large numbers of presses were in operation: in Venice, for example, about 150. The case was far different in Constantinople under the Ottomans. Although the non-Muslim population of the city could, and gradually did, take advantage of the new technology, it was forbidden to Muslims. In 1515, indeed, the sultan issued a decree which threatened any Muslim who attempted to learn the science of printing with the death penalty.

There may have been plausible, indeed compelling, reasons for this prohibition. The 'ulamā, or religious scholars of Islam, argued that to print the Koran would be sacrilege. The word of God must be transmitted only by 'the hands of scribes' (see the passage quoted from the Koran in Chapter 1), employing the finest calligraphy of which they were capable. Yet the contrast between the cultures of Christendom and of Islam in this matter of printing carries symbolic weight. The Dār al-Islām was unwilling to learn from Christendom; the disdain which had always been there was as strong as ever. But there is a little more to it than that. Consider the contrast with the early Abbasid period. Then, as we saw in Chapter 2, Muslim scholars grasped avidly at the learning of Greek and Persian antiquity, absorbed it, and enlarged and developed it. In the fifteenth and sixteenth centuries, on the other hand, there was a reluctance to embrace novelty, a sort of cultural failure of nerve. This withdrawal from intellectual receptivity is the more curious because it was coincident with the immense burst of confidence born of military triumph and political expansion, not simply in the Ottoman west of the *Dār al-Islām* but also (let us not forget though it has no part in this book) to the east in the shape of the Mogul Empire in India. Why was it that the scholars and scientists of the Ottoman period were less open, less adventurous, than their counterparts of the early Abbasid age? It is a question that has never convincingly been answered.

The continuance of an aloofness from European Christendom during the later Middle Ages may be illustrated from the lives of two near-contemporary natives of north Africa. Ibn Bāṭūṭah (d. 1378) was one of the most tireless travellers who ever lived. From the age of twenty-one for the succeeding thirty-odd years he was almost uninterruptedly on the move. He made the *hajj*, the pilgrimage to Mecca, four times. He visited the central Islamic lands in Syria, Mesopotamia and Persia. He crossed Central Asia to visit Afghanistan, India, China, Java, Sumatra and Ceylon. He dipped south by way of Oman to the coasts of East Africa. He went north to sample the Black Sea, the Crimea and the Volga basin. He knew Asia Minor, Egypt, his own North Africa of course, and al-Andalus in the far west. He crossed the Sahara to Timbuktu and the kingdom of Mali. Towards the end of his life he dictated an account of his travels based on the copious notes he had taken and his own retentive memory. The most authoritative English translation of Ibn Bāṭūṭah's travels occupies five volumes. In short, we know a great deal about him and his wanderings and there is no hint that it ever occurred to him in the course of them to visit European Christendom. Indeed, the casual readers of Ibn Bāṭūṭah's pages would scarcely be aware that there existed anywhere to the north of the Mediterranean.

My second example is Ibn Khaldūn (1332–1406). An eventful career as civil servant and diplomat acquainted him with the Islamic world from Spain to Syria. He encountered rulers as diverse as Pedro the Cruel of Castile and Tamerlane. He earned unpopularity as a *qāḍi*, or religious judge, in Cairo for his attempts to eliminate corruption from the workings of the law. He experienced misery when his family perished in a shipwreck. As an historian Ibn Khaldūn displayed an original and penetrating intelligence. His great contribution to the study of history lay in the emphasis he laid on what today would be called 'environmental' causation. His fundamental insight was that habitat – landscape, climate, ecology – has effects upon the culture, broadly defined, of the humans who live in it. The observable social phenomena, he further argued, obey trends which are sufficiently constant to yield regular patterns and sequences. The diligent enquirer can identify laws governing social development which are operative in societies of similar type, however separate from one another these societies may be in place or time. Ibn Khaldūn's starting point as an historian was a fascination with the interplay between the rugged interior and the fertile coastlands of his native North Africa; between the desert and the sown, the herdsman and the cultivator, the nomad and the settled. In studying these interactions he evolved a theory which he was confident could be employed as a key to understanding the reciprocities between, let us say, the pre-Islamic Arabs and the settled empires of antiquity, or the Bedouin of the Maghrib and the Spaniards they repeatedly invaded, or the Mongols and the agrarian societies they encountered.

Ibn Khaldūn's historical insights remain for the most part as fresh and as thought-provoking today as when they were first penned six centuries ago. He was one of the world's few great historical thinkers. But what is notable in the present context is that his observations were confined to the *Dār al-Islām*, to a single civilization, however diversely textured. (It is fair to say that he did also consider the territorial predecessors of the Islamic world, for instance the Persian Empire.) In a revealing aside in his great work the *Muqaddimah* [Preliminary Discourses] he let drop that he had 'heard rumours' that philosophy and science were flourishing in Christian Europe: 'but God knows best what goes on in those parts'.[3] No more than Ibn Bāṭūṭah did Ibn Khaldūn want to know about the Christian West.

Are there any examples at all of Islamic interest in Christendom from the fourteenth and fifteenth centuries? Only one. It is contained in the encyclopaedic work of Rashīd al-Dīn devoted to the history of the Mongols and composed about the year 1300. Because he wished to include brief accounts of the peoples with whom the Mongols came into contact, it was necessary to say something of the Europeans ('the Franks'). This he did by attaching to his text a translation of a chronicle composed by a Polish Dominican named Martin of Troppau who died in 1279. It is assumed that this text had made its way to Persia, where Rashīd was writing, in the baggage of one of several Western envoys. Martin's chronicle was a bald and summary work, but it was at once all that Rashīd had and all that he needed. He made no attempt to integrate it into his text, and left no hint that he was remotely interested in what Martin had to convey. It was a matter of literary convention: something had to be said about these barbarous people; let's get it over quickly. The very cursoriness of Rashīd's 'venture in occidentalism', as Bernard Lewis has called it,[4] simply underlines the lack of interest which Islamic scholars took in the West.

In Christendom, by contrast, there was eager interest in the *Dār al-Islām*. It was an interest which ran in several different channels, now convergent, now separate. There was the shocked horror provoked by apostasy. Anselmo Turmeda, a native of Majorca who was a Franciscan friar and a well-known poet, defected to Islam in the early fifteenth century. Subsequently he lampooned Christianity in a mocking work which drew upon the writings of Ibn Ḥazm. It was all extremely vexing and embarrassing. There was the fascination with, drifting into cautious admiration of, the might and efficiency of the Ottoman Empire. Gentile Bellini's celebrated portrait of Muhammad II is a sympathetic rendering: a Renaissance despot of recognizable type in Turkish costume. Machiavelli would admiringly ponder the springs of Ottoman power in his notorious handbook of advice for rulers, *Il Principe* [The Prince], composed in 1513. Ottoman dominion could even be presented as legitimate and glorious, as in a Latin panegyric to Muhammad II composed by the humanist Giovanni Filelfo in the 1470s, who claimed the Turks as descendants of the Trojans, rightful heirs to Asia Minor which had been stolen from them by the Greeks. Filelfo's patron was a merchant of Ancona who sought commercial favours from the Sultan; so flattery was the order of the day. Nevertheless it is a remarkable testimony to how far it was perceived that one might go in accommodating the Ottomans within a world-view. Academic study of the *Dār al-Islām* reasserted itself. In the course of the sixteenth century European collectors of Arabic manuscripts would make their appearance. Presses for printing in Arabic script would be developed. Chairs in Arabic would be founded in European universities. How delighted Ramón Lull or John of Segovia would have been! These scholarly preoccupations would continue and grow more robust in the seventeenth century and beyond. A final channel of interest was that of romance: the Muslim world as colourful, exotic, perilously attractive. When Ferdinand and Isabella formally took possession of Granada in 1492 in a moment that defined and completed the Christian reconquest of Spain, they chose to dress for the occasion in Moorish costume. Assuming the very garments of your defeated foe could be interpreted simply as a gesture of triumphalism. But this penchant for dressing up was also a continuation of a fashion which had been dominant at the court of Isabella's much-maligned half-brother and predecessor, Henry IV of Castile. Moorish clothes were high chic for the Spanish nobility in the age of the conquest of Granada, as were also Moorish cosmetics, horsemanship, falconry, architecture and interior decoration – many of the trappings of aristocratic life. Visitors to Ottoman Istanbul would soon be returning with whispers of sexual freedoms forbidden in the West, tales of harem and seraglio, of slave-markets and eunuchs, of brutal punishments meted out in sumptuous surroundings, to pander to the prurient fantasies of Europeans. Orientalism, as identified and vilified in Edward W. Said's book of that title published in 1978, did not have to wait upon Napoleon's expedition to Egypt. Its origins may be discerned three centuries earlier.

6

Epilogue

In 1321, the year in which Sanudo presented his *Liber Secretorum* to the pope, there were widespread rumours that the emir of Granada and the Mamlūk sultan of Egypt were plotting to poison the wells of France and Spain, using Jews and lepers as their network of agents. A generation later, in 1347–51, the horrendous visitation of the Black Death wiped out perhaps a third of the population of Europe: there were some who blamed it on Muslim agency. Suspicions of and accusations about chemical and biological warfare are not an invention of our own day.

In 1484, just as the war for Granada was gaining momentum, the Christian *and Muslim* blacksmiths of Segovia got together to found a confraternity or guild named after St Eligius, the patron saint of metalworkers, dedicated to the Virgin Mary 'and all the saints of the court of heaven'.

These examples alert us to certain kinds of perception, certain kinds of reality. On the one hand we have the Muslim as enemy, operating through a sinister network of health terrorists, or as scapegoat for the worst demographic disaster ever to overwhelm Europe. On the other we have one of those sparsely documented glimpses of what appear to be harmonious social relationships across religious and cultural boundaries which were probably fostered by craft or trade or calling. By a happy chance the example comes from John of Segovia's home town. We need to insert the words 'certain kinds of' because not all perceptions were like those of 1321 or 1350, not all realities like that of 1484. 'Alī of Daroca might have got on famously well with his workmates for all we know, but it didn't save him from being lynched when suspected of carnal relations with Prima Garsón. Wherever and whenever we direct our gaze we find a diversity in the type or the temperature of encounter. Perhaps the only safe generalization is also a blinding revelation of the obvious: the relations between Christian and Muslim during the Middle Ages were marked by the persistent failure of each to try to understand the other. It is easy to deplore this without making the effort to investigate why it should have been so.

Christian–Muslim relations took the form that they did because attitudes could not have been other than what they were. Christians first encountered Muslims as conquerors: it is readily intelligible that they should have perceived Islam as inherently martial. Given the intellectual and religious climate of the age, the only manner in which Christians could explain Islam in a fashion convincing to themselves was as an aberrant form of Christianity. There you have the two essential ingredients of the Christian image of Islam: Muhammad as a pseudo-prophet, impostor, heretic; his followers as men of blood and violence. Other elements would be added, for instance accusations of self-indulgence and sexual licence, but these two would always be the principal ones. They were already present in what seems to be the earliest record of Christian reaction to Islam, the *Doctrina Jacobi* quoted in Chapter 1, composed perhaps as early as 640 or so. The resultant image has proved quite remarkably long-lasting.

Muslims were from the first imbued with the supreme self-confidence born of the conviction that they had been chosen to receive God's last and most complete revelation; necessarily, therefore, they looked upon Christians with scorn. In addition, the *Dār al-Islām* occupied, by God's mercy and providence, a more favoured portion of the earth's surface than did Christendom. Seen from Baghdad in, say, the year 900, the Christian world was a jumble of confused sects and petty monarchies squirming about in an unappealing environment. The Islamic community had no rival in its wealth, its technology, its learning and its culture as well as in its faith. A lofty disdain was the only intelligible attitude for Muslims to adopt towards Christians.

Attitudes laid down like rocks long ago continue to shape their moral environment for many centuries thereafter. There is a geology of human relationships which it is unwise to neglect.

Most historians working today are sceptical of a way of arranging the past which sees a tract of time called 'the Middle Ages' as drawing to a close somewhere round about the year 1500. Yet in the history of the relations between Christians and Muslims that approximate date does have symbolic value, marking as it does the opening of that age of exploration in the course of which Europeans rediscovered Asia and India and found worlds new to them in the Americas and Africa. During the seventeenth and eighteenth centuries a European world hegemony would be constructed which rested upon economic dominance, institutions of government, military might and mastery of communications. Dramatic reversals of power would occur. The Ottoman Empire was the most powerful state in the world in the sixteenth century; by 1800 it continued to exist only because the European powers could not agree about what to put in its place. The *Dār al-Islām* was bullied, exploited and degraded by the arrogant westerners and experienced its deepest humiliation in the nineteenth and twentieth centuries. This in turn fuelled resentments which are still with us.

This European hegemony did not spring into being from nowhere during the early modern period. Its sinews and muscles were long developing, obscurely, in the recesses of western Christendom's being, as what we call the Middle Ages ran their course. To demonstrate this still insufficiently appreciated point would require another book. Suffice it for the present to observe that the striking economic, institutional and scientific advances of the period between the tenth and thirteenth centuries together formed the plinth on which later developments rested. During those formative medieval centuries western Christendom showed a capacity to develop, to change itself, in a manner which would underpin and facilitate all sorts of later changes. One facet of this process of self-development we have looked at briefly in Chapter 4. The intellectual advances of the twelfth and thirteenth centuries were achieved in large part by acquiring what the Islamic world had to offer. The pathway from Adelard of Bath to Isaac Newton is a long one, but it is clearly marked.

Muslim aloofness from Christendom had the effect of obscuring from view what was afoot. If travellers like Ibn Bāṭūṭah had visited Christendom they might have observed what was going forward: but they didn't. If Ibn Khaldūn had turned the piercing beam of his intelligence upon the societies of Western Europe he would have found much to ponder: but he didn't. The rise of the West took the world of Islam by surprise. Given Islamic disdain for the West, perhaps it had to happen thus.

Islam had of course shown a capacity to develop and to change itself too. The unsophisticated zealots who carried the Prophet's message and warning into the Roman and Persian worlds turned themselves into the mandarins of Baghdad, the merchants of Cairo or Aleppo, the scholars who propelled intellectual exploration into uncharted territories. It all happened so quickly too, in a matter of just a few generations. One cultural identity was exchanged for another. Such an extraordinary feat of moral redrafting or self-invention required a cultural suppleness, an adaptability, which seemed to run out in later epochs. Why did this happen? That question prompts this writer to return to the opening few paragraphs of Chapter 1; but the reader who has got thus far will probably just want to close the book instead.

Chronology

c. 570	Birth of the Prophet Muhammad.
622	Hegira of Muhammad from Mecca to Medina: beginning of Islamic chronological era.
632	Death of Muhammad.
634–43	Muslim conquest of Syria, Iraq, Egypt and Libya (635 Damascus; 637 Ctesiphon; 638 Jerusalem; 642 Alexandria; 643 Tripoli).
661	Foundation of Umayyad caliphate at Damascus.
674–8	First blockade of Constantinople.
698	Muslim conquest of Carthage.
c. 710	Construction of Umayyad mosque in Damascus.
711–18	Muslim conquest of Spain.
716–18	Second blockade of Constantinople.
730	Iconoclasm becomes official policy in the Eastern Roman Empire.
c. 750	John of Damascus dies.
750	Abbasid caliphate supplants Umayyad.
756	Umayyad prince becomes independent ruler of Córdoba.
762	Foundation of Baghdad.
768–814	CHARLEMAGNE.
778	Battle of Roncesvalles.
786–809	HĀRŪN AR-RASHĪD.
827	Muslim invasion of Sicily.

846	Muslim raid on Rome.
851–9	'Martyr movement' in Córdoba.
867	Al-Kindī dies.
873	Hunayn ibn Isḥāq dies.
910	Foundation of Fatimid caliphate in north Africa.
922	Ibn Faḍlān visits the Rus.
953–5	John of Gorze's embassy to Córdoba.
c.965	Gerbert of Aurillac studying in Spain.
969	Foundation of Cairo as capital of Fatimid caliphate. Byzantine conquest of Antioch.
972	Saracen pirates dislodged from La Garde-Freinet.
c.980	Seljuk Turks begin infiltration of the eastern Islamic territories.
c.990	First record of Italian merchants in Egypt.
997	Muslim sack of Santiago de Compostela.
1031	Disintegration of caliphate of Córdoba into *taifa* principalities.
1037	Ibn Sīnā (= Avicenna) dies.
1048	Al-Bīrūnī dies.
1055	Seljuk Turks capture Baghdad.
1060	Norman invasion of Sicily.
1064	Ibn Ḥazm dies.
1071	Byzantine army defeated by the Seljuk Turks at the Battle of Manzikert.
1082	Venetians acquire trading privileges in Constantinople.
1087	Pisan raid on al-Mahdīyya, Tunisia.
1088–91	Almoravid takeover of al-Andalus.
1090	'Abd Allāh of Granada exiled to Morocco.
1094	Rodrigo Díaz, El Cid, conquers Valencia.
1095	Pope Urban II preaches what would become known as the First Crusade.
1099	Crusaders conquer Jerusalem.
c.1100	*Digenes Akrites* and the *Chanson de Roland* committed to writing.

1118	Aragonese reconquest of Saragossa.
1142	Peter the Venerable commissions the translation of the Koran into Latin.
1144	Zengi reconquers the crusader state of Edessa for the Muslims.
1147	Portuguese reconquest of Lisbon.
1147–9	Second Crusade.
c.1150	Adelard of Bath dies.
1174–93	SALADIN.
1177	Pope Alexander III sends an embassy to Prester John.
1187	Battle of Hattin: Saladin reconquers Jerusalem. Gerard of Cremona dies.
1188	Usāmah ibn Munqidh dies.
1190–92	Third Crusade.
1198	Ibn Rushd (= Averroës) dies.
1202–4	Fourth Crusade.
1204	Rabbi Moses Maimonides dies. Conquest and sack of Constantinople by Western crusading armies.
1204–61	'Latin' Empire of Constantinople.
1212	Muslim forces defeated by Alfonso of Castile at the Battle of Las Navas de Tolosa.
1218–21	Fifth Crusade.
1227	GENGHIS KHAN dies.
1236	Castilian reconquest of Córdoba.
1238	Aragonese reconquest of Valencia.
1248	Castilian reconquest of Seville.
1248–50	Crusade of Louis IX of France.
1253–5	William of Rubruck's embassy to the Mongols.
1258	Mongol sack of Baghdad.
1260	Mongols defeated by Mamlūks at the Battle of 'Ayn Jālūt.
1271–95	Travels of Marco Polo.
1274	Thomas Aquinas dies.
1291	Acre, the last fragment of Outremer, falls to the Mamlūks of Egypt.

1292	Roger Bacon dies.
1311	Arnold of Vilanova dies.
1315	Ramón Lull dies.
1321	Dante dies.
1326	Osman, founder of the 'Ottoman' principality, dies.
c.1330	Pegolotti compiles his handbook for merchants.
1340	Merinid invasion of Spain: defeated at the Battle of the Rio Salado.
1343	Marino Sanudo dies.
1344	Crusaders conquer Smyrna; Castilians capture Algeciras.
1347–51	The Black Death.
1354	Ottomans conquer Gallipoli.
1365	Peter I of Cyprus raids Alexandria.
1378	Ibn Bāṭūṭah dies.
1389	Ottomans defeat local Christians at the Battle of Kosovo.
1396	Crusade of Nicopolis.
1402	Tamerlane's campaign in Asia Minor.
1406	Ibn Khaldūn dies.
1415	Portuguese conquest of Ceuta.
1453	Ottomans conquer Constantinople.
1458	John of Segovia dies.
1464	Nicholas of Cusa dies.
1492	Castilian reconquest of Granada.
1517	Ottomans annex Egypt.
1520–66	SULAIMĀN THE MAGNIFICENT.
1521	Ottomans conquer Belgrade.
1526	Hungarians defeated by Ottomans at the Battle of Mohács.
1529	First siege of Vienna.

Further Reading

This is in no sense a formal bibliography. I have sought simply to list some of the books which I have found useful and stimulating, and which a reader who is coming new to this topic might enjoy. I have deliberately limited myself to a very few items per chapter, having long been convinced that the value of a reading list is in inverse proportion to its length. I have confined myself to works in English.

Introductory and General

Of the many excellent introductory accounts of Islam, the best in my judgement is Bernard Lewis, *The Arabs in History*, first published in 1950, now in its sixth and fully revised edition (Oxford, 1993). Among more elaborate accounts Ira M. Lapidus, *A History of Islamic Societies* (Cambridge, 1988) is readable and sharp. *The Cambridge Illustrated History of Islam*, edited by Francis Robinson (Cambridge, 1996) is a recent collaborative work with rich accompanying illustrations. *The Legacy of Islam*, another collaborative work edited by Joseph Schacht and J. Bosworth (Oxford, 1974), contains essays on various facets of Islamic history and culture. The cultural encounter which forms the subject of the present book is the focus of a short and brilliant work by R. W. Southern, *Western Views of Islam in the Middle Ages* (Cambridge, Mass., 1962) and of a larger and looser study by Norman Daniel,

The Arabs and Medieval Europe (London, 1975). Because the Mediterranean is the setting for so many of the interactions which I consider here, it is appropriate to draw attention to Peregrine Horden and Nicholas Purcell, *The Corrupting Sea*: *A Study of Mediterranean History* (Oxford, 2000), the first volume of an elaborate and thought-provoking study of the Mediterranean world in antiquity and the Middle Ages.

Works of Reference

Three outstanding works of reference are (1) the *Encyclopedia of Islam*, and it is essential to consult the New Edition (Leiden, 1960 onwards) which has now (June 2002) reached the letter U and so is nearly complete; (2) the *Dictionary of the Middle Ages* in thirteen volumes under the general editorship of Joseph R. Strayer (New York, 1982–9); (3) the *Oxford Dictionary of Byzantium*, edited by A. Kazhdan and others (Oxford, 1991).

For the historical geography of the *Dār al-Islām*, William C. Brice, *An Historical Atlas of Islam* (Leiden, 1981) is recommended.

1. Ishmael's Children

There are innumerable introductory studies of the Prophet Muhammad: I single out Michael Cook's *Muhammad*, in the 'Past Masters' series (Oxford, 1983), for its succinct scholarship, its accessibility, and its sensitivity to its theme. All surveys of early Islamic history deal with the expansion of the faith: for example Francesco Gabrieli, *Muhammad and the Conquests of Islam* (London, 1968). Norman Daniel, *Islam and the West: The making of an image* (Edinburgh, 1960), provides a detailed investigation of evolving Christian attitudes to Islam. The best introduction to Islam in Spain is provided by Roger Collins in his *Early Medieval Spain: Unity in diversity 400–1000* (2nd ed., London, 1995); those who get intrigued by the problems could move on to his *The Arab Conquest of Spain 710–797* (Oxford, 1989).

2. An Elephant for Charlemagne

For the chronological framework, two books by Hugh Kennedy may be recommended: *The Prophet and the Age of the Caliphates: The Islamic Near East from the sixth to the eleventh century* (London, 1986) and *Muslim Spain and Portugal: A political history of al-Andalus* (London, 1996). For the Eastern Roman Empire see Mark Whittow, *The Making of Orthodox Byzantium 600–1025* (London, 1996). Richard Hodges and David Whitehouse, *Mohammed, Charlemagne and the Origins Of Europe: Archaeology and the Pirenne thesis* (London, 1983) is a reliable guide (though it deserves updating) to the debate about the economic effects of Islamic expansion. Richard Fletcher, *Moorish Spain* (London, 1992) and Thomas F. Glick, *Islamic and Christian Spain in the Early Middle Ages: Comparative perspectives on social and cultural formation* (Princeton, 1979) study the interactions between the two cultures in the Iberian Peninsula.

3. Crossing Frontiers

Michael Angold, *The Byzantine Empire 1025–1204* (London, 1984) is the best introduction to its theme. Books on the Crusades are legion: a good starting point is the collaborative volume edited by Jonathan Riley-Smith, *The Oxford Illustrated History of the Crusades* (Oxford, 1995), with its splendid illustrations. Carole Hillenbrand, *The Crusades: Islamic perspectives* (Edinburgh, 1999) breaks new ground. Richard Fletcher, *The Quest for El Cid* (London, 1989) is an attempt to place the hero of the Spanish *Reconquista* in context. David Morgan, *The Mongols* (Oxford, 1986) is a first-rate account of its complex subject; and for the larger context of exotic travel see J. R. S. Phillips, *The Medieval Expansion of Europe* (2nd ed., Oxford, 1998).

4. Commerce, Coexistence and Scholarship

Robert Bartlett, *The Making of Europe: Conquest, colonization and cultural change 950–1350* (London, 1993) is superb on the general context. David Nirenberg, *Communities of Violence: Persecution of minorities in the Middle Ages* (Princeton, 1996) is subtly illuminating on the inter-communal relationships of Jews, Christians and Muslims in the Aragonese dominions. Charles Burnett, *The Introduction of Arabic Learning into England* (London, 1997) elegantly charts one zone of intellectual transmission. Michael R. McVaugh, *Medicine before the Plague: Practitioners and their patients in the Crown of Aragon 1285–1345* (Cambridge, 1993) is a revelation, and so too on a different though related subject is Peter Biller, *The Measure of Multitude: Population in medieval thought* (Oxford, 2000).

5. Sieving the Koran

James Muldoon, *Popes, Lawyers and Infidels: The Church and the non-Christian world 1250–1550* (Philadelphia, 1979) surveys the attitudes of authority. Norman Housley, *The Later Crusades 1274–1580* (Oxford, 1992) deals with the Nicopolis Crusade of 1396 (among much else). Claude Cahen, *Pre-Ottoman Turkey* (London, 1968) and Halil Inalcik, *The Ottoman Empire: The classical age 1300–1600* (London, 1973) are excellent introductions to the Ottomans and their predecessors. Angus MacKay, *Spain in the Middle Ages: From frontier to empire 1000–1500* (London, 1977) is a brilliant short introduction to its theme. For more detail J. N. Hillgarth, *The Spanish Kingdoms 1250–1516* (2 vol., Oxford, 1976, 1978) is the standard work on later medieval Spain and Portugal. Peter Russell, *Prince Henry 'the Navigator': A life* (London, 2000) is full and convincingly iconoclastic. For the wider setting Felipe Fernández-Armesto, *Before Columbus: Exploration and colonisation from the Mediterranean to the Atlantic 1229–1492* (London, 1987) is learned, lively and readable.

Notes

Wherever possible I have directed readers to the most accessible English translation; where no published translation is acknowledged the translation is my own.

1. Ishmael's Children

1. Ammianus Marcellinus, *Res Gestae*, xiv.4, trans. J. C. Rolfe (Loeb Classical Library: Cambridge, Mass., 1935).
2. Isidore of Seville, *Etymologiae*, IX.ii.57, ed. W. M. Lindsay (Oxford, 1911).
3. Koran 80:11–15, as translated in A. J. Arberry, *The Koran Interpreted* (Oxford, 1964).
4. Koran 34:3, ibid.
5. Quoted in translation by P. Crone and M. Cook in *Hagarism: The making of the Islamic world* (Cambridge, 1977), pp. 3–4.
6. All Bede's references to the Saracens have been collected in the notes to *Venerabilis Bedae Opera Historica*, ed. C. Plummer (Oxford, 1896), vol. II, p. 339.
7. Ibid.
8. Ibid.
9. Koran 29:45, translated in A. J. Arberry, *The Koran Interpreted*.
10. Willibald, *Hodoeporicon*, translated by C. H. Talbot in *The Anglo-Saxon Missionaries in Germany* (London, 1954), pp. 162–3.
11. John of Damascus, *Dialogus*, translated by M. S. Seale in

Qu'ran and Bible: Studies in interpretation and dialogue (London, 1978), p. 70.

12. Section on the heresy of the Ishmaelites in *On Heresies*, trans. Frederic H. Chase Jr in *John of Damascus: Writings* ('Fathers of the Church' series: New York, 1958), p. 153.

13. Quoted in translation ibid., p. xiv.

14. *Chronicle of 754*, Chapter 78, translated by Kenneth B. Wolf in *Conquerors and Chroniclers of Medieval Spain* (Liverpool, 1990), p. 141.

15. Ibid., Chapter 70, p. 138.

16. *Ystoria de Mahomet*, translated by Kenneth B. Wolf in 'The Earliest Latin Lives of Muhammad' in *Conversion and Continuity: Indigenous Christian communities in Islamic lands, eighth to eighteenth centuries*, ed. M. Gervers and R. J. Bikhazi (Toronto, 1990), pp. 97–9.

17. Ibid.

2. An Elephant for Charlemagne

1. Quoted in translation by W. Z. Haddad in 'Continuity and Change in Religious Adherence: Ninth-century Baghdad' in *Conversion and Continuity: Indigenous Christian communities in Islamic lands, eighth to eighteenth centuries*, ed. M. Gervers and R. J. Bikhazi (Toronto, 1990), p.49.

2. Quoted in translation by Sidney H. Griffith in 'The First *Summa Theologiae* in Arabic: Christian Kalam in ninth-century Palestine' in *Conversion and Continuity*, ed. Gervers and Bikhazi, p. 19.

3. *Vita Iohannis abbatis Gorziensis*, Chapters 122–3, translated by Colin Smith in *Christians and Moors in Spain* (Warminster, 1988), vol. I, pp. 65–7.

4. Ibid.

5. Quoted in translation by D. J. Sahas in 'The Art and non-Art of Byzantine Polemics: Patterns of refutation in Byzantine anti-Islamic literature' in *Conversion and Continuity*, ed. Gervers and Bikhazi, p. 65.

6. Arculf, *De Locis Sanctis*, ii.28, trans. Denis Meehan (Dublin, 1958), p. 99.

7. Constantine Porphyrogenitus, *De Administrando Imperio*, Chapter 13, ed. Gy. Moravcsik with English translation by R. J. H. Jenkins (Budapest, 1949), p. 69.

8. Mark Whittow, *The Making of Orthodox Byzantium 600–1025* (London, 1996), p. 124.

9. *The Letters of Gerbert*, no. 25, trans. Harriet P. Lattin (New York, 1961).

10. Thomas N. Bisson, *Fiscal Accounts of Catalonia under the Early Count-Kings (1151–1213)* (Berkeley, 1984), vol. II, no. 162, lines 11, 188 (pp. 290, 294).

11. Henri Pirenne, *Mohammed and Charlemagne* (London, 1939), p. 234.

12. Quoted in translation by Gwyn Jones in *A History of the Vikings* (Oxford, 1984), p. 165.

13. Asser, *De Rebus Gestis Ælfredi*, ed. W. H. Stevenson (Oxford, 1904), Chapter 81, p. 68.

14. Quoted in translation by Robert S. Lopez and Irving W. Raymond in *Medieval Trade in the Mediterranean World* (New York, 1955), p. 54.

15. Ibid., p. 58.

16. Ibid.

3. Crossing Frontiers

1. Constantine Porphyrogenitus, *De Administrando Imperio*, Chapter 21, ed. Gy. Moravcsik with English translation by R. J. H. Jenkins (Budapest, 1949), p. 92.

2. *Digenes Akrites*, trans. John Mavrogordato (Oxford, 1956), Book V.

3. Ibid.

4. Ibid.

5. Ibid.

6. Ibid.

7. Ibid., line 3,511, p. 215.

8. *The Tibyan: Memoirs of 'Abd Allāh ibn Buluggin, last Zirid Amir of Granada*, trans. Amin T. Tibi (Leiden, 1986). pp.130–31.

9. *The Song of Roland*, trans. D. D. R. Owen (London, 1972), line 1,015.

10. Karen Armstrong, *Islam: A short history* (London, 2000), p. 81.

11. *The Crusade of Richard Lion-Heart, by Ambroise*, trans. Merton J. Hubert and John L. La Monte (New York, 1941), lines 10,267–79.

12. Jean de Joinville, *Life of St Louis*, trans. M. R. B. Shaw (Harmondsworth, 1963), p. 262.

13. *Gesta Francorum et aliorum Hierosolimitanorum*, trans. Rosalind Hill (Edinburgh, 1962), p. 21.

14. Joinville, *Life of St Louis*, p. 245.

15. Ibid., p. 305.

16. Quoted in translation by Francesco Gabrieli, *Arab Historians of the Crusades* (London, 1969), p. 73.

17. *The Mission of Friar William of Rubruck*, trans. Peter Jackson and David Morgan (Hakluyt Society: London, 1990), pp. 72–3.

18. Ibid., p. 158.

19. Joinville, *Life of St Louis*, p. 315.

4. Commerce, Coexistence and Scholarship

1. Quoted in translation by Felipe Fernández-Armesto in *Before Columbus: Exploration and Colonisation from the Mediterranean to the Atlantic 1229–1492* (London, 1987), p.152.

2. Quoted in translation by L. P. Harvey in *Islamic Spain 1250–1500* (Chicago, 1990), p. 56.

3. Sancho IV, *Castigos e Documentos*, Chapter 21, quoted in translation by J. N. Hillgarth in *The Spanish Kingdoms 1250–1516* (Oxford, 1976), vol. I, p. 213.

4. Ysa Yabir, *Breviario*, quoted in translation by David Nirenberg in *Communities of Violence: Persecution of minorities in the Middle Ages* (Princeton, 1996), p. 136.

5. Subtitle of Louise Cochrane's *Adelard of Bath* (London, 1994).
6. Quoted in translation by P. P. A. Biller in *The Measure of Multitude: Population in medieval thought* (Oxford, 2000), p. 255.
7. Quoted in translation by M. McVaugh in 'Arnald of Villanova', *Dictionary of Scientific Biography* (New York, 1970), vol. I, p. 290.
8. Quoted in Thomas E. Burman's translation by Olivia R. Constable in *Medieval Iberia: Readings from Christian, Muslim and Jewish sources* (Philadelphia, 1997), p. 83.
9. Quoted by M. Th. d'Alverny in 'Deux traductions latines du Coran au Moyen Age', *Archives d'Histoire doctrinale et littéraire du moyen âge* 16 (1948), p. 101, note 4.

5. Sieving the Koran

1. Quoted in translation by Philip Mansel in *Constantinople: City of the world's desire 1453–1924* (London, 1995), p. 25.
2. Quoted in translation by Peter Russell in *Prince Henry 'the Navigator': A life* (London, 2000), p. 15.
3. Quoted in translation by Bernard Lewis in 'The Muslim discovery of Europe' in his volume of essays *Islam in History* (London, 1973), p. 99.
4. Ibid.

Index

The following abbreviations are used in the index: Abp – Archbishop; Bp – Bishop; Cal – Caliph; Emp – Emperor; K – King; Pch – Patriarch; R – River; St – Saint;

PENGUIN HISTORY

BLOODFEUD: MURDER AND REVENGE IN ANGLO-SAXON ENGLAND   RICHARD FLETCHER

'Fletcher writes with precision and wit ... *Bloodfeud* dazzles and delights'
Sunday Times

'Fletcher writes convincingly and with distinction; as a storyteller, he carries his theme of murder and revenge at a cracking pace'
Iain Finlayson, *The Times*

In March 1016 Earl Uhtred of Northumbria was ambushed and brutally murdered by a rival magnate – with the full collusion of England's ruthless new ruler, King Canute – setting in motion a sixty-year cycle of violence, treachery, slaughter and revenge. In this gripping work of historical detection, Richard Fletcher sheds new light on the fledgling Anglo-Saxon world, and on legendary figures such as Ethelred the Unready, Eric Bloodaxe and William the Conquerer, bringing one of the most bloodthirsty periods of English history to life.

'A beautifully written gem, showing how the pattern of great events may be read in lesser ones, how brutal and sophisticated were the lives of our forebears' Alan Judd, *Sunday Telegraph*

'Enthralling ... confirms the historical perception of this dark millennial century as a succession of pitched battles between villainous gangs hell-bent on plunder ... a compelling work of forensic historical reconstruction' Mathilda Lisle, *Observer*

'Irresistible ... Fletcher has taken the quarrel as a framework and clothed it with a thorough and detailed examination of England in the tenth and eleventh centuries' Fiona Hook, *Independent on Sunday*

PENGUIN HISTORY

INFIDELS: THE CONFLICT BETWEEN CHRISTIANITY AND ISLAM
ANDREW WHEATCROFT

'Deeply impressive, well-informed and rich in detail ... unflinchingly examines the bloody faultline between Islam and the West' Martin Bright, *Observer*

'Imaginative, thought-provoking. Wheatcroft combine[s] martial history with analysis of hatred and misunderstanding' Jonathan Falla, *Scotland on Sunday*

'The kind of investigation Wheatcroft excels at. Events and their background are never as one sided as older, cruder narratives imply' *Independent*

'Wheatcroft has surveyed the centuries of Christian-Muslim conflict with meticulous care. It is gripping, often blood-curdling, history, and recounted with tremendous literary flair. A very good book' John Adamson, *Sunday Telegraph*

'Vivid ... Wheatcroft's account of the great sieges of the Crusades rivals Beevor's histories of the battles of Stalingrad and Berlin. *Infidels* is essential reading for anyone interested in what is happening in the new world order and how it could be reproducing a very old world order' Iain MacWhirter, *Sunday Herald*

'Detailed, disquieting, absorbing' A. C. Grayling, *Financial Times*

'Vivid and readable ... uses a sweep of scholarship and sources to narrate the enmity, fanned almost from Muhammad's death, between Christianity and Islam' Michael Binyon, *The Times*

'Entertaining, rattling good reading. Wheatcroft's conclusion is admirable' Felipe Fernandez-Armesto, *Sunday Times*

PENGUIN HISTORY

REFORMATION: EUROPE'S HOUSE DIVIDED
1490–1700 DIARMAID MacCULLOCH

'A magisterial and eloquent book. Diarmaid MacCulloch is uniquely able to communicate the religious passions of the past to the unbelief and indifference of the present' David Starkey

The Reformation and the Counter-Reformation it provoked are one of the great discontinuities in European and world history. The dramatic changes that began when Martin Luther nailed his ninety-five theses to the door of Wittenberg Cathedral in 1517 were of a different order to anything that had gone before. In the following two hundred years, the Western Christian world broke apart and the nature not just of European religion, but also of politics, thought, society and culture all changed utterly. The course of history down to our own time has been decisively shaped by this revolution.

Diarmaid MacCulloch's magnificent new history is the most authoritative and wide-ranging account of these epochal and often bloody events. He brilliantly describes the changing late medieval world into which Luther, Calvin and the other reformers erupted. He proposes an original new understanding of the often confusing origins of the exceptionally violent disagreements that divided men and women of the sixteenth and seventeenth centuries – disagreements for which they were prepared to kill and be killed.

But this is not simply a book about popes, scholars and reformers, religious battles and secular powers. MacCulloch examines the impact of the Reformation on everyday lives. He shows the power of ideas to ruin lives and rebuild them: to bring hope, fear, love, hatred, laughter, anger and joy to the humblest as well as the most exalted places in our continent.

RELIGION

ISLAM IN THE WORLD   MALISE RUTHVEN

'A clear and readable account of a large and complex subject'
Martin Hinds, *The Times Literary Supplement*

Islam is now recognised as a central political force in the modern world.
Malise Ruthven's acclaimed book is an essential introduction to the
Islamic world – past and present – and to the challenges it presents today.
Fully revised for this edition, it includes chapters on the spiritual richness
of the religion, the law and how it reflects attitudes to society and to
women in particular, as well as an incisive analysis of various Muslim
sects, their links and conflicts. A substantial new chapter discussed such
issues as the Rushdie affair, the reinterpretation of the doctrine of jihad to
encompass terrorism, and the internal strife that countries such as Algeria,
Iran, Israel and Egypt are experiencing, bringing this stimulating analysis
up to the present day.

'His exposition of the "Quranic world-view" is the most convincing, and
the most appealing, that I have read, and his observations about the
development and effects of Islamic law are original and thought-
provoking' Edward Mortimer, *The Times*

'A very readable book which may be offered with profit to the general
reader. Its chief merit is to reflect upon the present in the light of the past
and to do it well' Ian Netton, *The Times Higher Education Supplement*

'An unusual book, full of original ideas and judgements based upon wide
reading and personal observation' Albert Hourani, author of *A History of
the Arab Peoples*

THE AUTHENTIC GOSPEL OF JESUS
GEZA VERMES

There can be no doubt that Jesus, 'a religious genius' as Geza Vermes describes him, lived and taught in Palestine some 2,000 years ago. The influence he has had is incalculable. How though can we distinguish between the doctrines shaped to the needs of the burgeoning Christian church and the original views laid out by the Master himself? How can we dig back through the additions, misinterpretations and confusions of later writers and two millennia of church tradition to return to the authentic gospel of Jesus?

In his new book, Geza Vermes subjects all the sayings of Jesus to brilliantly informed scrutiny. Profoundly aware of the limits of our knowledge but immersed in what we do have – both the 'official' gospels and associated Jewish and early Christian texts – Vermes sieves through every quote ascribed to Jesus to let the reader get as close as possible to the charismatic Jewish healer and moralist who changed the world. The result is a book that creates a revolutionary and unexpected picture of Jesus – scraping aside the accretions of centuries to come as close as we can hope to be to his true teaching.

PRAISE FOR *THE CHANGING FACES OF JESUS*

'A masterly statement of a great scholar who has spent decades considering his topic and whose work is gentle, ironic, relatively unargumentative, and written with exceptional skill' E. P. Sanders, *New York Review of Books*

'A magnificent achievement . . . a constant delight . . . this is a comprehensive, definitive and sympathetic portrait' David Goldberg, *Independent*

'A masterpiece' A. N. Wilson, *Daily Mail*

PENGUIN HISTORY

A HISTORY OF THE MIDDLE EAST
PETER MANSFIELD, revised and updated by
NICOLAS PELHAM

SECOND EDITION

'A brilliantly deft and well-informed guide ... coherent, dispassionate and remarkably inclusive' *The Times Educational Supplement*

'An excellent political overview' *Guardian*

Over the centuries the Middle East has confounded the dreams of conquerors and peacemakers alike. In this profound book, Peter Mansfield follows the historic struggles of the region over the last two hundred years, from Napoleon's assault on Egypt, through the slow decline and fall of the Ottoman Empire, to the painful emergence of modern nations, the Palestinian question and Islamic resurgence. The Middle East's huge oil reserves gave it global economic importance as well as unique strategic value, and the result was massive superpower involvement.

For this new edition, Nicolas Pelham has written two extensive new chapters examining recent developments throughout the Middle East since the Gulf War, including the turbulent events in Afghanistan, the troubled relationship between the US and Iraq, the continuing Arab-Israeli war and the rise of Islamic Jihad.

Incisive and illuminating, *A History of the Middle East* is essential reading for anyone wishing to understand what is perhaps the most crucial and volatile nerve centre of the world, and its prospects for the future.

'The best overall survey of the politics, regional rivalries, and economics of the contemporary Arab world' *Washington Post Book World*

NATASHA'S DANCE: A CULTURAL HISTORY OF RUSSIA   ORLANDO FIGES

THE TOP TEN BESTSELLER FROM THE AUTHOR OF
A PEOPLE'S TRAGEDY

'Wonderfully rich ... magnificent and compelling ... a delight to read'
Antony Beevor

'Awe-inspiring ... *Natasha's Dance* has all the qualities of an epic tragedy'
Frances Welsh, *Mail on Sunday*

Orlando Figes's enthralling, richly evocative history has been heralded as
a literary masterpiece on Russia, the lives of those who have shaped its
culture, and the enduring spirit of a people.

'A *tour de force* by the great storyteller of modern Russian historians ...
Figes mobilizes a cast of serf harems, dynasties, politburos, libertines,
filmmakers, novelists, composers, poets, tsars and tyrants ... superb,
flamboyant and masterful' Simon Sebag Montefiore, *Financial Times*

'It is so much fun to read that I hesitate to write too much, for fear of
spoiling the pleasures and surprises of the book' Anne Applebaum,
Sunday Telegraph

'Magnificent ... Figes is at his exciting best' Robert Service, *Guardian*

'Breathtaking ... The title of this masterly history comes from *War and
Peace*, when the aristocratic heroine, Natasha Rostova, finds herself
intuitively picking up the rhythm of a peasant dance ... One of those
books that, at times, makes you wonder how you have so far managed to
do without it' Robin Buss, *Independent on Sunday*

'Thrilling, dizzying ... I would defy any reader not to be captivated'
Lindsey Hughes, *Literary Review*

PENGUIN HISTORY

EMPIRE, WAR AND FAITH IN EARLY MODERN EUROPE GEOFFREY PARKER

'Masterful ... to travel in Parker's company is always stimulating and illuminating' Felipe Fernandez-Armesto, *Sunday Times*

In this brilliant and provocative study, renowned historian Geoffrey Parker traces the rise and fall of global empires, the impact of mass warfare and limits to religious growth in sixteenth- and seventeenth-century Europe. He ranges from the dramatic rise and fall of Philip II's Spanish superpower to William of Orange's invasion of England; from Elizabethan espionage and treason to the spread of Protestantism; from the development of military technology to war crimes and the 'etiquette of atrocity' in early modern Europe. All reveal what the short-lived triumphs and devastating failures of this period can tell us about today's world.

'One of the most distinguished historians of early modern Europe. He staggers his readers by the depth of his learning and by the width of his subject matter, which ranges from the sexual obsessions of the Scottish Kirk to the treatment of American Indians' Raymond Carr, *Spectator*

'Dazzling ... absorbingly readable' Noel Malcolm, *Sunday Telegraph*

'In this age of ever-intensifying specialization and ever-increasing publication, merely keeping abreast of early modern European political history *and* military history *and* the history of religion would seem a truly superhuman task. Geoffrey Parker is one of the few people who possesses such superhuman capacities. These are models of historical essay-writing' Noel Malcolm, *Sunday Telegraph*

'The finest military historian currently writing' Jeremy Black

PENGUIN HISTORY

SPAIN'S ROAD TO EMPIRE: THE MAKING OF A WORLD POWER 1492–1763   HENRY KAMEN

'Brilliant . . . lucid, scholarly and perceptive . . . a revelation'
Peter Preston, *Observer*

How did an impoverished, thinly populated country, isolated from the rest of Europe, become the world's first superpower?

Henry Kamen's superb book sheds fascinating new light on Imperial Spain's journey to power, from the capture of Moorish Granada to the opening up of the frontiers in Texas and California. Drawing on extensive research and eye-witness accounts, he overturns our traditional view of the all-conquering enemy of Protestant Europe, demonstrating that the Spanish Empire was above all a global, collaborative venture, which depended as much on the cooperation (willing or otherwise) of native Americans, Africans and Asians as that of Europeans for its success. It was, he argues, this diversity of resources and peoples that made Spain's impact on world history so overwhelming.

'The best as well as the boldest existing book on the subject . . . This is salutary revisionism, which Kamen tackles with his usual virtues: forthright language, vigorous pace, vivid examples, resilient thinking, critical intelligence, robust scholarship, uninhibited audacity . . . At last Henry Kamen has given us a history which . . . looks at "the untold story"'
Felipe Fernandez-Armesto, *Literary Review*

'A splendid new book' Paul Kennedy, *Guardian*

'Kamen, an expert on imperial Spain . . . pulls off a considerable achievement. He changes our perception of the Spanish empire'
Ann Wroe, *Daily Telegraph*